GARLAND STUDIES ON

INDUSTRIAL
PRODUCTIVITY

edited by

STUART BRUCHEY
ALLAN NEVINS PROFESSOR EMERITUS
COLUMBIA UNIVERSITY

A GARLAND SERIES

GENDER AND SUCCESSFUL HUMAN RESOURCE DECISIONS IN SMALL BUSINESSES

DEBORAH CAIN GOOD

GARLAND PUBLISHING, Inc.
A MEMBER OF THE TAYLOR & FRANCIS GROUP
NEW YORK & LONDON / 1998

Library of Congress Cataloging-in-Publication Data

Good, Deborah Cain, 1958–
    Gender and successful human resource decisions in small
businesses / Deborah Cain Good.
        p.   cm. — (Garland studies on industrial productivity)
    Includes bibliographical references and index.
    ISBN 0-8153-3170-3 (alk. paper)
    1. Small business—Personnel management. 2. Women-
owned business enterprises.   I. Title.   II. Series.
HF5549.G647 1998
658.3'03—dc21

                                                                98-9420

Printed on acid-free, 250-year-life paper
Manufactured in the United States of America

Dedicated to Mom, Dad and John
whose unending support
provides me the time to be me.

Contents

List of Tables

ix

List of Figures

xi

Preface

The growth of small business in the United States over the past decade has been explosive. Fueled by the changing roles of women in society and a structural shift in the nature and types of businesses, the numbers of small businesses, revenues generated by them and employment opportunities offered in them continue to increase. In stark contrast to the public recognition of this growing economic sector, however, is the decided lack of information on the basic practices of these firms. Particularly absent is data on necessary human resource practices carried out in small businesses.

This book is an attempt to better understand the human resource programs utilized by small firms and the basis for their choice. Much of the study is designed to provide a working framework from which to begin to understand the myriad of human resource decisions made in these companies on a daily basis. In this way the research seeks to make some contribution to the development of a theoretical grounding for human resources in the small business area.

The research in this book originates from my doctoral dissertation at the University of Pittsburgh. During the course of research for my doctorate, I sought and received the cooperation and advice of the directors of a number of diverse groups directly or indirectly associated with small business. Though too numerous to mention, I offer my sincere appreciation to them for their time and attention. Their energy and strong belief in the importance of small business is characteristic of all my contacts in the area. My experiences lead me to believe the potential for growth and opportunity in this economic sector is substantial.

Acknowledgments

I would like to thank James Craft for his invaluable advice while writing this book and his careful reading of and advice on the many drafts of the study on which it is based. I am also grateful to Donna Wood, John Prescott, Jim Klingensmith and Gary Florkowski for their many critiques and suggestions on various sections.

I am indebted to the Small Business Development network and The National Education Center for Women in business for their advice and ready participation in this endeavor. My parents, Robert and Joan Cain, deserve special thanks for their uncanny ability to recognize when physical, emotional or intellectual support is needed; may I someday acquire that skill. A final thank you to John, Jennifer and Mike who are always there for me.

Gender and Successful
Human Resource Decisions
in Small Businesses

CHAPTER 1
Introduction

Small businesses are a critical part of the U.S. economy. In 1993, they employed close to 60 percent of the work force, generated 54 percent of the sales and were responsible for over 40 percent of gross domestic product. From 1987 to 1992, small and midsize firms created all of the 5.8 million new jobs in the U.S. economy. Meanwhile, companies with 500 or more employees recorded a net loss of 2.3 million jobs for the same period. In addition, small firms produce twice as many innovations per employee as large firms. In short, small business is a major innovator, economic force and job creator in today's marketplace.

THE RESEARCH PROBLEM

The continued vitality of this economic sector, however, requires a renewed focus on increasing productivity, and improving employee and managerial skills. Such prescriptions require an understanding of the types of human resource programming utilized by small business owners. Although those in the human resource management area have shown a great interest in developing human resource strategy to support the firm's competitive business strategy as a means to accomplishing organizational objectives and gaining competitive advantage, surprisingly little is known about human resource practices in the small business sector.

This dearth of knowledge is especially surprising given the exponential growth of the service sector over the past few years, a sector characterized by small, labor intensive firms where, seemingly, human resource policies will have a short term, direct impact on the firms' performance. On the other hand, simple observation suggests that even within the same industry (e.g. retailing) firms pursue a wide array of human resource programs, plans, policies and practices. Even though much attention has recently been paid to small business at various levels of government and in the popular press, few efforts have made to bring some sense of order to the diversity in human resource practices utilized in the sector. This study will begin to provide some insight on these issues so as to identify those human resource strategies which are the most successful in the small business area.

The logical starting points for such an endeavor are the existing management models which have been formulated in the corporate setting. One such model, from the strategic management field, examines the alignment or "fit" of internal and external variables in a firm. For example, a "fit" between competitive business strategy and the context of the firm should lead to positive performance for that firm.

This study will be the first to examine the same relationship in the small business setting in spite of arguments made by some scholars that small businesses do not have competitive business strategies or that their human resource practices are not sophisticated.[1] Yet, all businesses, even "Mom and Pop shops", make some type of selection, compensation, training and development decisions. While the model developed from an examination of corporations may not be entirely appropriate for small businesses, until a new one is created, the former serves as an adequate baseline from which to begin to find out exactly what occurs in the small business with regard to human resources.

The alignment model calls for an assessment of the relationships between internal and external variables within a system. Even in the small business area, there are a maddening number of variables and relationships between them to investigate. Assessing which of those variables directly determines another and which simply influence others is a formidable task. However, once again, the corporate setting can offer some hints on where to begin to examine the determinants of human resource strategy in the small business setting. Research conducted in large corporations has suggested that competitive business strategy is the primary determinant of human resource strategy.[2] Thus, competitive business strategy will be the initial focus of this study.

Equally important and unique to this study, will be an assessment of the impact of the contextual factor of owner gender on the competitive business and human resource strategies of small businesses. In contrast to the corporate setting where upper level leadership and ownership are heavily male dominated, the small business arena boasts a decided female influence.

The investigation of the impact of business owner gender on the practices of the business is especially important in the small business setting given the contributions of women-owned firms to the sector. Small businesses as a whole are increasing in numbers, with women-owned enterprises responsible for a substantial portion of that overall increase. In fact, government statistics indicate that the annual growth rate of women-owned businesses more than doubled that of male-owned firms during the 1979-1989 period.[3] Yet, the similarities and differences between the two are only now beginning to be investigated with little comprehensive data on women-owned businesses from which to start.[4] Indeed, gender may influence aspects of human resource strategy ranging from the choice of business to the overall effectiveness of the firm.

RESEARCH QUESTIONS

This study will seek to provide preliminary answers to the questions:

1. What types of human resources strategies are found in small businesses?
2. Does gender influence the type of human resource strategy chosen by a small business?
3. Is the choice of human resource strategy related to a small business' performance?

PURPOSES OF THE BOOK

The goals of this research are:

1. To define and measure the concept of human resource strategy;
2. To examine the relationships between human resource strategy and its chief determinant, competitive business strategy;
3. To examine the relationship between a demographic characteristic, gender, and human resource strategy; and
4. To assess the relationship between human resource strategy and firm performance.

THE NATURE OF THE STUDY

This research project was conducted in four phases. Phase one was an in-depth interview with small business owners regarding their human resource practices.[5] Phase two was the content analysis of company documents supplied by those business owners.[6] The analysis was designed to assess the types of human resource practices formally recognized in the firm. The third phase of the study was the pre-test of a questionnaire developed from an extensive literature review of the area and the outcomes of phases one and two.[7] The project's final phase was a large scale questionnaire study of small business owners to ascertain their human resource strategies.[8]

A wide variety of small business support groups[9] readily offered their advice and resources to facilitate the completion of this study. The directors' help was solicited in securing membership listings as well as in identification of small businesses which might participate in either phase one or three of the project. Given the nature of such sampling, this project is cross-industry in character.

Firms are identified as "small businesses"[10] for the purposes of this study if they meet the following criteria:

1. Management by individual managers where managers are also the owners.
2. Capital supplied and ownership held by an individual or small group.
3. Area of operations mainly local with workers and owners being from the home community. However, markets for the products need not be local.
4. The size in the industry is small relative to the largest unit in that field.

ORGANIZATION OF THE BOOK

This book is the culmination of two years of case study and survey research in the small business area. The research project it describes was originally designed to be a detailed examination of human resource strategy whose chief contribution was as an academic definition in the human resource area only. However, a serendipitous research project introduced the author to the small business area. And, as they say, "the rest is history". A few minor adjustments of the originally conceived research design and the study has become one of potential to small business owners and those interested in gender-based issues in the area.

Chapter 1, the Introduction, describes, in general fashion, the background, research problem and research questions that are the basis of this study.

A review of relevant literature is presented in Chapter 2. This chapter combines information from the strategic management, human resource, small business and gender studies areas to create the background for this project. In addition, the development of the study's model, and the definition and manner of measurement of relevant terms is also presented.

Chapter 3 details the assessment of human resource priorities within the small business. The nature of such priorities and their relationship to competitive business strategy, gender and financial performance is highlighted.

Human resource decisions related to programs and practices is presented in Chapter 4. Again, patterns in human resource programming in relation to competitive business strategy, gender and financial performance are examined as they appear in the sample of small businesses participating in the study.

The final chapter of this dissertation, Chapter 5, discusses the implications of the study's findings. Study findings are interpreted as to their impact on public policy makers and academics. The significance of the research findings and the limitations of this study are also discussed.

NOTES

1. Miller and Toulouse (1986) argue that small businesses do not have competitive business strategies. Huselid (1993b) used an index created by the Department of Labor to measure the sophistication of human resource practices. He determined that, in general, human resource practices are not highly sophisticated in most small businesses.

2. Researchers reaching this conclusion include Wils and Dyer (1984), Dyer (1984), DeBejar and Milkovich (1986b) and Buller, Beck-Dudley and McEvoy (1990).

3. Refer to *The State of Small Business, 1992,* for a full discussion of statistics on the growth of women-owned businesses in the United States during this time period.

4. From the annual report to the President, *The State of Small Business, 1992*, p.50.

5. Fifteen small business owners participated in the initial case study phase of this project. The businesses were located in the southwestern Pennsylvania region. The industries represented by the 15 firms interviewed include: electrical products, high technology, manufacturing, health care, and food service. The number of individuals employed by the firms ranges from 23 up to 201 with a median of 76 employees and a mean of 107 employees per firm. Mean sales (billings) of the firms is $1.7 million per year with the range of sales extending from $450,000 to $100 million annually and a median sales level of $1,940,000. The oldest firm studied in this phase was established in 1954, the most recent was created in 1989. The mean age of the firms interviewed was 14 years, the median 9 years. Accordingly, the firms are small businesses but generally not in their introductory stages. In all cases the firms are owner-managed establishments.

6. Interviews averaged one and one-half hours in length although three of the fifteen were two hour interviews and one stretched to three hours. The structured questionnaire used in the interviews appears in Appendix 1. Appendix 2 contains the format for analysis of those interviews. All fifteen participants requested complete anonymity in the publication of this document. Accordingly interview quotations are presented throughout the text of this document with only a general identification of the individual making the statement.

In an attempt to secure a more national sampling for the project a heavy focus was placed on gaining the assistance of Small Business Development Centers (SBDCs). Under the direction of the Pennsylvania SBDC director, the other state SBDC directors were contacted by phone to describe the project and request their assistance in the survey. Thirty three directors expressed an interest in the project, and a follow-up letter detailing our phone conversation was sent to their attention. Ultimately, twenty-two SBDCs throughout the country participated in the project. Each SBDC was requested to secure five respondents for the study, although some centers requested a lower level of participation and others requested a higher level. Figure 1.1 shows the geographic distribution of participants secured by SBDCs across the country.

During the course of the interviews, company documents were requested of each business owner. Seven of the fifteen participants supplied such documents. The format used in analyzing company documents appears in Appendix 3. Due to requests for confidentiality in the use of those documents, no segments of them will be reproduced here.

7. Given the information collected in the first two phases of this project, a questionnaire was developed for pilot testing. Twenty one firms participated in this phase. The firms were found in the following industries: electrical products, high technology, light manufacturing, manufacturing products, health services, food products, and food services. The number of individuals employed by these firms ranged from 17 to 191 with the mean being 98 and the median 71. The mean sales (billings) of the firms was $1.3 million per year with a range from $250,000 to $50 million and a median of $6.4 million. The mean age of the pre-test firms was 11 years with the earliest being established in 1963 and the most recent start-up in 1990. The median age of the firms is 17 years.

Following completion of the pretest, participants were interviewed about their impressions of the survey. One key finding of the pilot test was that the amount of time required to complete the questionnaire was excessive for small business owners. Accordingly, the focus of this inquiry was tightened on the core relationships between competitive business strategy, human resource priorities and human resource programs. This increased attention to a smaller number of core relationships led to a refinement of the original questionnaire. Specifically, inquiries as to the small business owner's managerial style and values were eliminated from the survey. The general direction of the research, however, remained intact.

8. 213 firms participated in the final, questionnaire phase of the project. Again all participating firms were small businesses located in the continental United States. One hundred nine of the firms were manufacturing oriented, and 104 service oriented. Figure 1.2 shows the number of firms in each line of business represented in the sample.

1993 sales (billings) for the firms ranged from $27,000 to $108,000,000. The mean sales for the 213 firms was $8,618,902, the median, $17, 900,000. The mean number of employees per firm was 48, the median 72, with the range from 9 to 451 individuals. The oldest firm in the sample was established in 1898, and the most recent in 1993. The mean firm age was 32 years old, the median 31.

The questionnaire took between 15 and 20 minutes to complete. Each questionnaire mailed to a possible participant was accompanied by (1) a letter of explanation regarding the project and assuring the respondent of anonymity and confidentiality and; (2) a business reply envelope.

9. Directors of the following groups were contacted prior to the start of this research project and their cooperation requested. The groups included small business development centers across the country, chapters of the National

Association of Women Business Owners, Area Chambers of Commerce, The National Education Center for Women in Business, and various specialty entrepreneurship organizations.

   10. It is beyond the scope of this study to add to the theoretical argument in the entrepreneurship field centered on the definition of an "entrepreneur" versus that of a "small business owner". Yet, this review would be remiss without a mention of the difficulties which arise from misuse of either term. Generally, the entrepreneur is viewed as one who is an innovator, endowing resources with new capacity for creating wealth, thereby creating resources. See Gartner, 1989 and 1990; Carland, Hoy, Boulton, & Carland, 1984; Hisrich & Brush, 1986; Brockhaus, 1987; Brockhaus & Horwitz, 1985; Sexton & Smilor, 1985; Ronstadt et. al., 1986, Low & MacMillan, 1988; Sandberg, 1992 and Wortman, 1985. The small business owner is not viewed as such a creator. The differentiation between the two definitions is not seen as vital for purposes of this study, and thus the terms will be used interchangeably here.

CHAPTER 2

Building the Human Resource Model

One of the many bedroom communities in Southwestern Pennsylvania offers its residents three independently owned and operated grocery stores which are not affiliated with any local or national grocery chains. Each store features enlarged delicatessen, bakery, greeting card and pharmacy sections. Each is open daily from 7 a.m. until 11 p.m. and both offer customers double coupon values. Three identical grocery stores? Not when the owners of each site are questioned as to their hiring, training and compensation practices. Instead, three very different pictures emerge as to how to deal with employees. To fully understand and appreciate the diversity, a framework is needed by which to organize and compare the practices used by the store owners. The strategic management and human resource areas offer such a model, albeit one created from a corporation perspective. Nonetheless, it proves a good starting point for examining the activities in the small business arena.

DEVELOPMENT OF THE MODEL

For the past two decades, strategy has been an important concept in management thought. Recently, those in the human resource management area have shown a great interest in developing human resource strategy to support the firm's business strategy as a means to accomplishing organizational objectives. Many management scholars argue the need to utilize human resources to gain a competitive advantage for the firm.[1] Nonetheless, human resource strategy remains one of the least understood of the factors that lead to success or failure in strategy implementation. The development of a clear definition of human resource strategy would facilitate such understanding.

KEY ELEMENTS OF HUMAN RESOURCE STRATEGY

Human resource researchers have used two general approaches in defining the concept of a human resource strategy. The first approach is to simply extend strategic management concepts directly into the human resource area. DeBejar and Milkovich (1986a) suggest that ". . . human resource strategy (HRS) is simply a special case of the more general definition of strategy . . ."[2]; one based on Hofer and Schendel's widely accepted definition of organizational strategy[3]. Thus the DeBejar and Milkovich definition of human resource strategy becomes, "a pattern in a stream of human resource (HR)-related decisions which may occur at various levels in the organization".[4] Similarly, Dyer (1984) states, "Borrowing from the strategy literature, we define organizational human resource strategy (OHRS) as the pattern that emerges from a stream of important decisions that indicate management's major goals and the means that are (or will be) used to pursue them".[5]

A second approach to defining human resource strategy is to view the concept in functional terms, that is, as a combination of human resource functions. Galbraith and Nathanson (1978) first introduced the concept of human resource value in the strategic management process. They suggested that human resources activities could be matched to an organization's strategies and structures. The pair saw four human resource functions as primary: selection, appraisal, rewards and development. Various combinations of organizational strategy and structure produced different combinations of the functions, in essence, different human resource strategies.

Fombrun, Tichy, and Devanna (1984) use the framework as a starting point for their work, but, go further, conceptualizing the functions as four separate control systems. They argue that each of the systems must be seen as a coherent whole in and of itself. Further, these systems must be fully integrated with one another as well as with other control systems (i.e. budgeting, planning and information systems) for the human resource strategy of the firm to take shape.

Miles and Snow (1984) also define a human resource strategy in terms of its functional parts. Using their business strategy typology (e.g. Defender, Prospector, Analyzer) as a starting point, they examined the role that human resources play in each organization. They argued that three human resource activities are common to all organizations— building, acquiring, and allocating. The priority assigned to each activity as well as its manner of performance differs in each organization in line with differences in strategy. They presented guidelines for developing effective human resource systems based on strategic type. Accordingly, Defender organizations concentrated on building human resources. Prospector organizations directed their human resource activities toward acquiring resources and finally, Analyzer types allocated their human resources.

Ferris, Schellenberg and Zammuto (1984) also view human resource strategies as functional in nature. In their analysis of human resource strategies in declining industries, the environmental niche of the declining industry was determined. Then, the human resource processes (recruitment and termination, training and development, evaluation, reward and retention for developmental purposes) or tools to create a human resource pool of competencies were discussed.

Hax (1985) defines a human resource strategy as a set of well coordinated objectives and action programs aimed at securing a long term sustainable advantage over the firm's competition. He places human resource activities into five categories to ensure their comprehensiveness (selection, promotion and placement, appraisal, rewards, management development, and labor/employee relations). Again the basis of the categories is functional.

Wright (1986) notes the problems in viewing human resource strategies through the traditional personnel functions: 1) it limits the alternative strategies an organization might choose, 2) it prevents seeing possible synergies or conflicts among human resource practices, and 3) it distorts the theoretical strategic change taking place. One further complication of the human resource strategy as function view, is that it is difficult to distinguish between the strategy itself and the determinants of that strategy.

Now that the importance of human resources to the competitive position of the firm is widely accepted managers have begun to examine the activities of their human resource departments. Human resource practices are looked at in isolation as well as in combination with each other, and the concept of a human resource strategy is beginning to emerge. Yet as the above sections indicate, no single operational definition of the concept exists. Shirley (1982) notes, "(t)here are almost as many definitions of strategy as there are writers about the subject".[6] The same statement could be made with regard to a definition of human resource strategy.

Consensus on a strategy definition is unlikely to exist because strategy is multidimensional as well as situational in nature.[7] Similarly, consensus is unlikely to exist on a definition of human resource strategy as well. While a single definition may not be possible, some degree of commonality across definitions is necessary for future theory development. The starting point must be the strategic management literature, where a thorough analysis of the dimensions of strategy has been completed. These dimensions can now be incorporated into the human resource field.

The main thrust of much of the strategic management literature is that there is a need for the firm to identify and then match internal strengths and weaknesses with external opportunities and threats to attain a "fit".[8] This "fit" is the chosen strategy. Thus, the definition of human resource strategy needs to address five key areas.

1) Level

Strategy is formulated and then applied at different levels. Hofer and Schendel (1978) propose a widely accepted three tier hierarchy of organizational strategy: Corporate, business unit and functional levels. Corporate level strategy defines the business in which the firm will operate. Business unit strategy answers the question: How will the firm compete in the chosen business? At the functional level, strategy deals with the day to day actions taken at the operational level of the business which maximize the productivity of resources.

2) Content vs. Process Orientation

Strategic management studies generally have one of two broad orientations: a concern with content issues or with process issues. Content studies rely on substantive elements for examination. Shirley (1982) notes that such studies traditionally deal with what decisions are made, under what conditions and why.

Process studies, in contrast, examine the functional aspects of decision making and problem formulation. Specifically, procedures, activities and methods are investigated.

3) Incremental vs. Rational Viewpoints

The rational or comprehensive process of strategy formulation (Grant & King, 1982) argues that there is a rational, analytical way to conduct problem solving. The emphasis is on the logical determination of goals, the evaluation of alternatives and the establishment of plans prior to action.

The counterpart of this approach is that of incrementalism. Logical incrementalism suggests that effective strategies emerge from a series of strategic subsystems.[9] As such strategy tends to evolve as a pattern in a stream of decisions.[10] Accordingly, strategy elements are examined to determine the resulting pattern.

4) Intended vs. Realized Strategies

Mintzberg and Waters (1985) argue that a gap exists between strategies that are intended and those that are actually realized within the organization. Intended strategies are those which are planned for and frequently documented by strategic planning groups. Realized strategies, on the other hand, are the actions and policies as they are actually implemented in the organization.

5) Scope

Scope refers to the inclusiveness of the strategy, specifically, whether strategy entails both ends (goals) and the means for achieving them.

To date, definitions of human resource strategy have addressed only two of these perspectives: content and level. Dyer (1984) adopts a decisional perspective in his work on the content of human resource strategy, examining the "important decisions about the management of human resources".[11] The level of human resource strategy is clearly addressed by DeBejar and Milkovich (1986a). In one of the first empirical studies of human resource strategy, the pair focus on the business unit level of human resource strategy. The other three areas, while certainly vital to a clear definition of human resource strategy, have either been completely overlooked (intended versus realized strategies), inferred (incremental versus rational viewpoints) or misused (scope).

If human resource practitioners are to become more viable members of the business organization, they must learn to think in a more strategic manner. Part of this learning process is fully understanding and utilizing the well established concepts of strategy in the human resource field, specifically by building a working definition of human resource strategy.

HUMAN RESOURCE STRATEGY ELEMENTS

Bourgeois (1980) notes ". . . Specifying the level at which the study is taking place would impose more conceptual rigor on the investigation.".[12] To date few human resource strategy studies have made a distinction in level even though Dyer (1984) called for descriptive research to be conducted at all three levels (corporate, business unit and functional) in an early agenda setting discussion of research in the area.

A study by Wils and Dyer (1984) distinguished between organizational level human resource strategy (OHRS) which covered the strategic management of human resources of all types and in all locations, and functional human resource strategy (FHRS) which covers the strategic management of personnel units. And, DeBejar and Milkovich (1986a; 1986b), focused on the business unit level of human resource strategy.[13]

Reflecting Hofer and Schendel's strategic hierarchy[14], this study establishes a distinction in the levels of human resource strategy. Specifically, business human resource strategy (BHRS) and functional human resource strategy (FHRS) will be examined.

Dyer (1984) adopts a decisional perspective in his work on the content of human resource strategy, examining the "important decisions about the management of human resources".[15] DeBejar and Milkovich (1986a; 1986b) also utilize the decisional perspective in their studies.[16]

Similarly this study will examine the content of human resource strategy at each level. Since "content is crucial to organizational performance,"[17] BHRS will focus on human resource decisions made for the business unit as a whole, encompassing all functional departments. This study will call these decisions human resource priorities. FHRS will focus on specific human resource program decisions. This study will call these decisions human resource activities. Past studies have not made such fine content and level distinctions. Instead measures at both levels have been used indiscriminately to assess human resources.[18] In addition, this differentiation between BHRS and FHRS addresses the three other perspectives pertinent to a clear definition of strategy.

BHRS is the intended goals the business has for human resources that will help the firm achieve a competitive advantage. These goals can be arrived at in a rational strategy formulation process where the relationship between the human resource strategy and, for example, the organizational business strategy can be assessed.

FHRS, on the other hand, is the means by which the business human resource strategy is implemented. Accordingly, FHRS is determined incrementally (often in hindsight) and represents the strategy as it is realized. (Figure 2.1 summarizes the elements of human resource strategy used in this paper.)

MEASURING THE HUMAN RESOURCE STRATEGY ELEMENTS

Human resource strategy has been defined and measured in a variety of ways. DeBejar and Milkovich (1986a; 1986b), propose that human resource strategy is made up of four components: domain, deployment, synergy and competitive advantage, which are assessed by seven dimensions:

Domain referred to key employee groups and key human resource activities.

Deployment was defined by human resource allocation or staffing decisions and investment in human resources.

Synergy referred to the effects the business achieved through the combination of all its human resource decisions; both operating and strategic.

Competitive advantage was measured as the human resource strengths the firm has in relation to its competitors.[19]

Sixty variables along these seven dimensions were developed for a questionnaire study of a random sample of SBUs from a list of Fortune 1000 and 50 largest corporations.

Wils and Dyer (1984) conducted an exploratory questionnaire study of 22 businesses within one corporation. The businesses represented several divisions of the firm operating in a variety of industries. Questionnaires were given to business unit managers and concerned the nature and management of their management teams. In this study human resource strategy consisted of three components:

> Organizational human resource strategy (OHRS) or the strategic management of human resources of all types and in all locations within the firm;
> Major human resource problems; and
> Functional human resource strategy (FHRS) or the strategic management of personnel units.[20]

OHRS was represented by decisions on employee utilization and allocation. Specifically questions were asked regarding quantity (manager headcount), quality (performance and promotion potential) and functional area competence (the rank order importance of several functional skills including marketing, manufacturing, sales, research and development, distribution, legal affairs, finance and production).

Human resource problems were measured via an open-ended question requesting managers to list the two most important personnel problems pertaining to the management of their management team over the past year.

Finally, FHRS was measured by the rank ordering of activities as to their importance in the solution of problems in managing the management team. These activities included: recruitment and selection for the acquisition of new managers or for the replacement of departing managers, replacement or career planning, performance appraisal, training and organization development.

Schuler (1987; 1989), uses strategic human resource management to explore the link between institutional and individual level concerns in industrial relations.[21] Human resource strategy, in this study, is defined by human resource utilization decisions and the actions of employers.

Schuler and Jackson (1989a;1989b) defined human resource strategy by two different components: role behaviors and human resource practices. Role behaviors are what is needed from an employee who works with other employees in a social setting. Role behaviors represent the key areas in which the human resource function can contribute to a firm's competitive strategy. Human resource practices, in contrast, are alternative choices within each functional area of human resource management (i.e., to utilize long term versus short term human resource planning techniques).[22] Based on the survey responses of a cross industry sample of 300 human resource managers,"menus"[23] of the practices were developed for planning, staffing, appraisal, compensation, training and development and labor-management relations.

This study will examine the concept of human resource strategy using two measures: human resource priorities and human resource activities. Human resource priorities are the primary human resource orientations or concerns of the firm.[24] These orientations are developed for the organization or business unit as a whole and thus represent business human resource strategy. It is to these concerns that the firm attaches the most importance. (Figure 2.2 presents examples of human resource priorities).

Human resource decisions are also made at a second level, within the human resource department. These decisions center around specific human resource functions and the ways these functions can be used to implement the human resource orientations laid out at the organizational level. This functional human resource strategy will be assessed by examining specific human resource programs and plans.[25]

In summary, business human resource strategy will be determined by the pattern of human resource priorities found within an organization. Functional human resource strategy is the pattern of human resource programs and plans implemented by a firm's human resource department.

Though no previous studies have made as fine content and level distinctions as these definitions do, others have offered varying degrees of specificity in their projects. Dwelling on such distinctions and spending so much time building a case for them from the literature may appear to be a purely academic pursuit, but it is instead designed to underscore the absolutely critical nature of this issue when played out in the actual workplace. Policies are set at one level in a corporation and the programs to implement them are often played out on yet another level. Or, in the case of the small business, the owner desires some behavior be exhibited by his employees and undertakes various programs to achieve it. Regardless of company size, coordination of the programs must be insured to prevent the sending of mixed signals to employees. This study's definition of human resource strategy strives to highlight the importance of these issues to the employee and the firm as a whole.

THE DETERMINANTS OF HUMAN RESOURCE STRATEGY

Now that the nature of human resource strategy in this study has been established, the variables impacting its configuration can be assessed. Again, the strategic management literature offers some direction. Early descriptive research suggested that competitive business strategy was the major determinant of human resource strategy.[26] DeBejar and Milkovich (1986b), using a multidimensional model in the first empirical study of human resource strategy, found that human resource strategy does vary systematically with business unit strategy.[27] More recent work in the small business area has further substantiated the link between competitive business strategy and human resource strategy.[28]

Competitive Business Strategy

Early studies assessing the linkage between organizational competitive strategy and human resource strategy were prescriptive in nature.[29] For example, Miles and Snow (1984) suggested that the human resource strategy should be designed to support the basic competitive strategy of the firm. Using their well-known typology to categorize three firms (Lincoln Electric, Hewlett-Packard, and Texas Instruments) by competitive strategy, the pair suggested that "(t)he human resources department should pursue appropriate strategies of its own to match the organization's business strategies".[30] Accordingly, Defender organizations would use a "build" human resource strategy, Prospectors would seek to "acquire" human resources and Analyzers would "allocate" human resources.

LaBelle (1983), after conducting case studies of eleven Canadian firms in four industries, concluded that organizational strategy was the chief determinant of organizational human resource strategy.[31] Clear differences in the configurations of organizational human resource strategies existed across firms with differing competitive strategies.

Wils & Dyer (1984) conducted a questionnaire study of 22 business units within one corporation. Although only one dimension of organizational human resource strategy was assessed, employee utilization and allocation, the results strongly suggested a link between the organizational human resource strategy and competitive strategy.

Each business unit's competitive strategy was assessed by use of a "strategic move position" based on the work of the Boston Consulting Group. The moves created three categories for business strategy: growth, profit and stabilization. Businesses pursuing a growth strategy tried to increase headcounts and improve the quality of their managers. In contrast, businesses pursuing a profit strategy showed little change with regard to headcount as well as maintaining or milking their managerial talent.

Milkovich and DeBejar (1986b), in one of the first empirical studies of human resource strategy, found a moderate but significant relationship between a business's competitive strategy and its human resource strategy. Data from 129 business units was collected via questionnaire and used to categorize firms into one of eight competitive strategy types (increasing market share, rapid growth, profit, operations turnaround, strategy turnaround, expansion, contraction and liquidation). Canonical correlations between business strategy and human resource strategy indicated a moderate but significant relationship. Further, using the business human resource strategy, business units were correctly classified as to their competitive strategy 84% of the time.

Small business research on the relationship between competitive business strategy and business human resource strategy is generally prescriptive in nature. However, Buller, Beck-Dudley, and McEvoy (1990) examined the linkages between human resource practices in law firms and the competitive strategies pursued. Using Porter's framework[32] as a basis for competitive strategy, a self-report questionnaire study of partners in a sample of 1000 law firms in 11 U.S. cities was done. The results indicate that different human resource practices are indeed associated with different competitive strategies. Specifically, those firms pursuing a differentiation strategy use selection systems that emphasize high levels of ability and experience, performance appraisal systems that are formal and emphasize the quality of work, compensation systems that emphasize high base salary, internal equity and individual and group incentives, and training and development systems that are highly supportive of employees.

In contrast, law firms pursuing cost leadership strategies use selection systems that emphasize ability, performance appraisal systems that are informal and emphasize quantity and quality, compensation systems with relatively low base salary, external equity and few incentives, and little emphasis on training and development.

Further, Bamberger and Phillips (1991) used content analysis to examine the annual reports of firms of varying sizes in the pharmaceutical industry. Their assumption was that competitive business strategy was the chief determinant of human resource strategy. This finding was substantiated given the specific human resource dimension examined.

Although empirical evidence for the link between competitive strategy and human resource strategy is limited, linkages of aspects of human resource strategy, most notably compensation strategy, have been investigated. Carroll (1987) provided a prescriptive link between elements of the compensation system and strategy. Specifically, he suggests that Defender firms use quantitative performance measures, individual bonuses, emphasize short run performance and gainsharing programs. Prospector firms, in contrast, use more qualitative performance measures, have large bonus payments, use merit bonuses generally for group work, and emphasize long run performance and deferred compensation. Newman (1987), also speaks from a prescriptive position, suggesting that incentive systems be tailored to complement the chosen organization strategy.

Broderick (1985)[33] used the Miles and Snow typology (e.g. Defender, Prospector, Analyzer) in an empirical examination of compensation strategies. The study looked at seven policies for determining middle management pay systems: external competitiveness, performance/membership, efficiency vs. growth, level of managers participating, level of managers approving decisions, standardization of plans across units, and formalization of written documents. Distinctly different patterns were found for Defender and Prospector organizations. Using discriminant analysis, the patterns were able to correctly identify organization type (Defender, Prospector) at a rate significantly beyond chance.

Balkin & Gomez-Mejia (1990) also examined the impact of organizational strategy on pay strategy. Based on survey responses of 192 human resource management executives in large manufacturing firms, corporate strategy was found to be a significant predictor of compensation strategy. Compensation strategy was defined in terms of three components: pay package design (the mix between salary, benefits and incentives); market positioning (relationship of pay level to that of competitors); and pay policy choices (the criteria and procedural approaches used to pay employees).

The most diversified firms tend to show higher pay levels, greater emphasis on salary and benefits in relation to incentives, greater formalization of pay procedures and a higher degree of pay secrecy. In contrast, the least diversified firms have lower pay levels, a greater emphasis on incentives in the pay mix, and more decentralized decision making in an open communication atmosphere. Using discriminant analysis, patterns of compensation policies were able to correctly classify business units by strategy, at a rate much better than chance. The simple conclusion drawn from these findings is that "management adjusts its pay strategies to fit with the organizational strategy".[34]

Other Environmental Factors

Although competitive business strategy is the primary determinant of human resource strategy, the presence of various internal and external environmental factors may moderate the relationship somewhat. In the internal environment, researchers have identified a number of factors which may impact the competitive business strategy-human resource strategy linkage. These factors include: management values, organizational structure, human resource strengths and weaknesses, management philosophy, internal labor markets and political and power bases.[35]

Researchers also suggest that variables in the external environment may influence the linkage. These variables include: life cycle phase, external labor markets, the presence or absence of a union and legislation.[36]

It is important to note however, that the internal and external environmental variables were identified from prescriptive research. Most of the studies did not adopt methodologies capable of distinguishing relative effects or lacked systematic data relating the factors to strategies. In contrast, empirical studies consistently indicate a relationship between competitive business strategy and human resource strategy.[37]

Semantic arguments aside, this study examines the competitive business-human resource strategy relationship when viewed in the small business sector with special attention to the gender of that business' owner. Again this is uncharted territory in small business/entrepreneurship research, but is designed to provide some preliminary ideas from which to begin theory development in the area.

Small Business Influences

Though debate continues on the job creating capabilities of small business, few argue that the sector plays a vital role in the U.S. economy. The Small Business Administration says there are approximately 21 million small businesses in the United States, employing close to 49.4 million individuals.

America is currently undergoing a major structural shift in its economy from a heavily manufacturing oriented one to an increasingly service oriented one. Traditionally service sector firms, by their very nature, tend to be smaller in terms of numbers of employees. Thus, as the structural shift continues, the numbers of small firms increase.

Accompanying the shift in industrial bases are shifts in the philosophy by which American businesses are run coupled with a changing mindset on the nature of the traditional family and family member roles. Both have focused attention on the value of small business. Specifically, downsizing actions on the part of many U.S. companies, designed to enhance efficiency and effectiveness in the firm, have caused many employees to lease their skills back to their former employer, ostensibly as a consultant. Often, leased employees "sell" their skills to other firms and readily become a functioning small business.

Women, traditionally viewed as the primary child care provider, are creating new roles for themselves by opening home-based businesses in record numbers[38]. Others are creating firms outside the home, stimulating changes in all family member roles. Whatever the scenario, the American dream is realized as increasing numbers of individuals become "their own bosses".

Even as the numbers of small businesses continue to grow, researchers question the nature of the enterprise and seek to develop a theory of its management. Numerous small business publications have thoroughly assessed the difference between small business and entrepreneurship. Others have devoted considerable attention to determining the presence of competitive business strategy in the small business or its predisposition to any type of planning.

Early studies on competitive strategy in the small firm focused on the type of planning performed. Two studies[39] looked at the incidence of strategic versus operational planning in small retail food firms and its relationship to performance. They found that those firms which systematically practiced both strategic and operational planning outperformed firms which did not do such planning. But, they also found that those firms which performed systematic operational planning only performed almost as well as those firms engaging in both types of planning. In fact, over 85% of the firms in the study's sample did not practice systematic strategic planning.

Lyles, Baird, Orris and Kuratko (1993) found small businesses with formal planning practices increased their growth rate of sales. Gable and Topol (1987) also examined the planning practices of small-scale retail stores. However, their findings suggest that planning has very little impact on sales or profits.

Such findings could suggest that small firms do not have competitive business strategies such as those offered by Porter (1980) and Miles and Snow (1978).[40] Many small business researchers argue that the cost leadership strategy, for example, would not be viable for a small business because of its inability to create and benefit from economies of scale.[41]

Such findings could also suggest that small firms are simply adopting strategies which are not conducive to high performance given their developmental stage and activities. Boeker (1989) notes that strategy in a firm can be inertial, that is, once a strategy is adopted, it is very difficult to change it. Therefore, small business owners may simply be pursuing the strategies that they initially chose for their firms because they are not able to quickly adapt to changing environmental conditions.

Developmental interviews for this study indicate that small business owners are very knowledgeable of the Porter competitive strategy typology (1980). Cost containment via economies of scale in the traditional manufacturing sense may not be realistic goals for small businesses, but economies of scale through cost reductions from experience in knowledge-based service activities and in other areas are possible.[42] Further, Variyam and Kraybill (1993), in a study of small businesses in Georgia, suggest that strategies in small business differ from those cited in large businesses. Specifically, small businesses tend to pursue planning, product strategies, the adoption of new technology and have a general concern for employee quality. In short, the Porter typology (1980)[43] while perhaps inadequate in describing the breadth of strategies pursued by small businesses, is certainly adequate as a general description of their competitive business strategy, and, as such, is adopted for this study.

Gender Influences

Any examination of small business would be incomplete without an accompanying analysis of gender effects in those firms. Within the small business segment, female-owned organizations currently are the prime impetus for growth. In 1992, businesses owned by women created more jobs than all of the Fortune 500 companies combined. Further, women-owned businesses grew at a rate more than twice that of male-owned firms.[44]

Yet, women face many more obstacles in establishing and managing their businesses than their male counterparts. Women face greater difficulties in gaining access to financial resources, have fewer recognized management and leadership skills and have greater family pressures and responsibilities than their male counterparts.[45] Moore, Buttner & Rosen(1992) note that research on female entrepreneurs is "fragmented, unrelated, at a descriptive level, and at best representing only an initial stage of paradigm development".[46]

For example, prescriptive research has long suggested a difference between the way women approach business matters and the manner in which men deal with the same issues. Given the fact that women have restricted access to such resources as financing and differing social networks the competitive business strategies they choose for their small businesses may differ from those chosen by their male counterparts.[47] Very preliminary studies indicate that women tend to avoid low cost competitive strategies, but, if they do choose to compete on that basis, are more likely to fail than their male counterparts.[48] This study will attempt to examine gender differences with regard to various factors in the conceptual framework.

ALIGNING THE MODEL ELEMENTS

Underlying the relationship between competitive business strategy and human resource strategy and other internal and external environmental variables, is the fundamental principle of "fit" from the strategic management area. The concept of "fit" goes by various names in the literature—alignment, coalignment, consistency, and contingency [49] and is rooted in various disciplines including business policy, industrial organization, economics, administrative behavior and marketing.[50] Regardless of the terminology used or the school of thought from which it derives, the concept calls for a match between a strategy and its context (indicated by either external or internal variables).

The external environment was the contextual focus of work by Andrews (1971), who called for the alignment of organizational resources with environmental opportunities and threats. Both Hofer (1975) and Anderson & Zeithaml (1984) looked at the match between business unit strategy and the external variable, product life cycle.

Context has also been viewed as an internal variable by various researchers. Chandler (1962) looked at the alignment between strategy and structure. Lorange and Vancil (1977) and Galbraith and Nathanson (1978) examined the match between strategy and administrative systems. Schwartz and Davis (1981) and Stonich (1982) focused on aligning the internal variable, culture, with strategy. Finally, Gupta and Govindarajan (1984) examined the "fit" between managerial characteristics and business unit strategy.

As Venkatraman and Prescott (1990) note: "In simple terms the proposition is that the "fit" between strategy and its context has significant positive implications for performance"[51]. Indeed, Venkatraman and Ramanujam (1986) suggest that business performance is at the heart of strategic management. As such, a number of researchers have conducted empirical studies of the impact of alignment on performance.

The studies assumed that the strategy formulation process is an attempt to align organizational resources with environmental opportunities and threats and that performance measures indicate the success of such a match. While Pearce, Freeman and Robinson (1987) note the methodological problems of these studies as well as their contradictory results, they still maintain the viability of studies assessing the performance impact various factors have.

One of the earliest and best known studies looking at whether firms employing formal strategic planning outperform firms without planning was one by Thune and House (1970). In a longitudinal investigation, they matched pairs of planners and nonplanners in 36 large manufacturing firms. Thune and House found that firms employing formal strategic planning in the drug, chemical and machinery industries outperformed nonplanners in measures of EPS, ROE and ROI. Formal planners in the steel, oil and food industries, however, showed no significant performance differences using the same measures.

A second early study (Ansoff et. al., 1970) also indicated that formal planners significantly outperformed their nonplanning counterparts. Ansoff, Avner, Brandenburg, Porter and Radosevich (1970) looked at the acquisition planning success of 22 firms using formal strategic planning methods versus 40 firms not using such methods. Twenty one objective measures of performance on thirteen variables were combined with subjective measures of success to arrive at a performance measure. The results indicated that extensive formal planners significantly outperformed firms that did little formal planning, most notably on sales and earnings growth rates.

Using research designs similar to these early studies, later work also indicated that use of strategic planning methods leads to enhanced performance. Herold (1972), using five matched pairs of planners and nonplanners in the chemical and drug industries, found that formal planners outperform informal planners in sales and profit measures. Matching 19 large planners and nonplanners in the chemical, drugs, electronics and machinery industries, Karger and Malik (1975) found that formal integrated long range planners outperformed informal planners on almost all of 13 economic measures including EPS and operating margin. Finally, Wood and LaForge (1979) looked at planners and nonplanners among large U.S. banks. Again comprehensive planners outperformed nonplanners with respect to ROE and growth in net income.

Conflicting results on the impact of planning were found by other researchers. Grinyer and Norburn (1974) conducted in-depth interviews with multiple respondents in 21 large United Kingdom firms. They found no relation between formal planning and financial performance (here measured as return on net assets). Similarly, Kudla (1980) looked at 78 planners and 51 nonplanners from a group of Fortune 500 firms. He found no evidence that strategic planning leads to improved returns even when such returns are adjusted for risk.

Perhaps most indicative of the mixed results of studies on the impact of formal planning on financial performance were those found by Rue and Fulmer (1973). The pair looked at 386 large firms in the durable, nondurable and service industries. In the durable goods industry, formal planners consistently outperformed nonplanners. No consistent relationship between planning and performance was found in the nondurable industry. The service industry, however, provided the most interesting results where nonplanners actually consistently outperformed planners on such measures as sales and earnings growth.

The lack of consistent results between strategic planning and financial performance has been attributed to design problems including the operationalization of "formal planning"[52] and the lack of a distinction in planning level. King (1983) argues that such studies take an indirect or "black box"[53] approach to strategic planning. That is, most studies treat the outcome of planning, the strategy, as a black box assessed by the ultimate performance of the business. Such an approach never provides for assessment of the nature or quality of the strategy.

To date, there has also been minimal attention in human resource research to data assessing the impact on performance of various human resource priorities or programming. Yet, Schuler and Jackson (1989a) note, ". . . a fit between human resource management practices and organizational strategy is likely to be more effective than a lack of fit . . ."[54].

Kerr (1985) notes the overall lack of research investigating the relationship between reward systems and competitive business strategies, as well the lack of information on relationships between human resource areas and strategy or performance. Zahra and Covin (1993) examined technology policy and found it to align with business strategy such that the technology policy's "fit with business policy is a significant predictor of firm performance."[55].

Schuler (1992) suggests a similar relationship between human resource strategy and competitive business strategy. He assessed the consistency between human resource practices and the business needs of Pepsi Cola International and found them to be in alignment.

Mosakowski (1993) examined 86 computer software firms to ascertain what competitive business strategies were being pursued in the firms. She found that in the firms where focus and differentiation strategies were established, performance is higher than in other firms.

In a more general sense, Naman and Slevin (1992), in a study of 82 manufacturing firms, found that "fit" is an important construct for firm success. Overall firm performance is positively related to the measure of "fit" in the firm. This study will attempt to provide some additional information on the concept of alignment in the small firm.

THE HUMAN RESOURCE STRATEGY MODEL

The conceptual framework that results from this literature is shown in Figure 2.3

The figure suggests that competitive business strategy is the chief determinant of human resource strategy. Human resource strategy is found at two levels within the firm. Human resource priorities are indicative of the business human resource strategy. Human resource programs, plans and policies suggest the functional human resource strategy. Both levels of human resource strategy can enhance performance in either the functional area or the overall firm. The model will be examined in the small business setting with gender effects considered.

The reader is reminded that many of the assumptions utilized in the formation of this model are developed from corporate research. Although some may prove inappropriate for the small business arena, until such time as they are disproved, they serve as a legitimate starting point for this project.

ALIGNMENT: A RESEARCH QUESTION

The underlying relationships depicted in this model suggest that firms utilizing similar competitive strategies should implement similar human resource programs. Yet, simple observation indicates a wide variety of programs and policies are used by firms operating in the same industry. Further, observation indicates that firms pursuing very different programming can be very successful. In light of this, this study will seek to examine the following research question:

> "Given a firm classified as an effective performer, what is the relationship between the human resource priorities used by that firm and the human resource programs utilized?"

This research question will be a preliminary examination of the concept of alignment. It is likely effective low cost (differentiation) performers will have an identifiable human resource priority profile. Effective low cost (differentiation) performers will also have a definable human resource program profile. Consistencies in the profiles across firms will signal some degree of fit or alignment between the two.

Schneider and Bowen (1993) examined the relationship between employee perceptions about service climate and human resource management experiences and customer service quality ratings. In all cases, they found a statistical correlation between employees' work attitudes and customer satisfaction. The pair cited numerous firms where large scale statistical studies on the same topic were ongoing, including Sears, NCR and Ryder. Schuler (1992) also found alignment at Pepsi Cola International given the consistency between its human resource practices and its business needs. Such empirical findings provide some evidence of the alignment concept, evidence that will be sought in this study.

NOTES

1. Among the many researchers making this argument are Dyer and Holder (1988), Schuler and Jackson (1989), Schuler and MacMillan (1984), Miles and Snow (1984), Swiercz and Spencer (1992) and Gould (1984).

2. DeBejar and Milkovich, "Human Resource Strategy at the Business Level: Study 1: Theoretical Model and Empirical Verification." Paper presented at Academy of Management Meetings, Chicago, 1986. p. 10.

3. Hofer and Schendel (1978) defined a strategy as the "basic characteristics of the match an organization achieves with its environment" (p.4). Further, the pair describes three levels of strategy: corporate, business and functional.

4. DeBejar and Milkovich (1986a): p. 4.

5. Dyer, "Studying Human Resource Strategy: An Approach and An Agenda." *Industrial Relations* 23(1984): p. 159.

6. Shirley, "Limiting the Scope of Strategy: A Decision Based Approach." *Academy of Management Review* 7(1982).

7. See Hambrick (1980) for a detailed description of the dimensions of strategy as well as its situational nature.

8. See Venkatraman and Prescott (1990), Venkatraman and Camillus (1984), Schendel (1990) and Hofer and Schendel (1978) for various discussions on the nature of internal and external environments and the concept of "fit".

9. Quinn (1980) develops the concept of logical incrementalism.

10. Mintzberg (1978) develops a classic definition of strategy.

11. Dyer, "Studying Human Resource Strategy: An Approach and An Agenda." *Industrial Relations* 23(1984): p. 159.

12. Bourgeois, "Strategy and Environment." *Academy of Management Review* 5(1980): pp. 27-28.

13. DeBejar and Milkovich (1986a, 1986b) describe the manner in which human resources can be measured at the business level.

14. Hofer and Schendel (1978) describe the three levels of strategy as corporate, business and functional.

15. Dyer, "Studying Human Resource Strategy: An Approach and An Agenda." *Industrial Relations* 23(1984): p. 159.

16. DeBejar and Milkovich (1986a; 1986b) explicitly describe the manner in which human resource practices were assessed in participating firms of their sample.

17. Bourgeois, "Strategy and Environment." *Academy of Management Review* 5(1980): p. 29.

18. See Schuler and Jackson (1989), Dyer and Holder (1988), and Wils and Dyer (1984) for a discussion of the lack of attention to level of decision making as well as an example of a study in which the level of human resource decision making is unclear.

19. See DeBejar and Milkovich (1986a) for specific examples of human resource decisions which fit each dimension.

20. Wils and Dyer (1984) provide examples of human resource decisions at various levels in the organization.

21. See Schuler and Jackson (1989) for a full description of the nature of role behaviors and human resource practices.

22. See Schuler and Jackson (1989) for a list of alternative choices in each functional area.

23. The "menus" presented in Schuler and Jackson (1989) have been used quite extensively by researchers to develop questionnaires for individual functional areas like staffing and training.

24. See Craft (1988) for another view on human resource priorities and their definition. Human resource priorities as used in this study more closely parallels the Schuler and Jackson (1989) model than the Craft (1988) version.

25. Schuler (1987; 1989) develops and refines the concept of human resource practices.

26. See Wils and Dyer (1984) and Dyer 91984) for a description of the study which suggests that competitive business strategy is a key determinant of human resource strategy.

27. See DeBejar and Milkovich (1986b) for specific results. Canonical correlation and regression were utilized.

28. See Buller, Beck-Dudley and McEvoy (1990).

29. Results in Milkovich (1988) and Dyer (1985) were based on case study evidence.

30. The pair used their famous Defender, Prospector, Analyzer paradigm to classify firms and then assessed the types of human resource strategies needed.

31. The study mentioned in Dyer (1984) was completed as part of an MBA requirement.

32. Porter (1980) developed the framework of generic competitive business strategies in his book, *Competitive Strategy*.

33. Broderick's (1985) study is discussed at length in Milkovich's (1988) piece.

34. Balkin and Gomez-Mejia (1990), p. 163.

35. These internal factors were identified in studies by Craft (1988), Dyer (1984, 1985), LaBelle (1983), Wils and Dyer (1984), Miles and Snow (1984), Milkovich (1988) and Osterman (1984).

36. The external environmental variables were examined in studies by Craft (1988), Dyer (1984), Smith (1982a), Balkin and Gomez-Mejia (1987), Anderson and Zeithaml (1984), Lewis (1963), and Freeman and Medoff (1984).

37. Including studies by Schuler and Jackson (1989), Dyer (1984; 1985), Milkovich (1988), and Dyer and Holder (1988).

38. According to the National Foundation for Women Business Owners, women-owned home-based businesses number 3.5 million and employ about 14 million people in the United States.

39. See Robinson, Salem, Logan and Pearce (1986) and Robinson, Logan and Salem (1986).

40. Porter's competitive business strategy typology features overall cost leadership, differentiation and focus strategies. Miles and Snow created the Defender, Prospector and Analyzer typology.

41. Researchers drawing this conclusion include Miller and Toulouse (1986), Chaganti, Chaganti and Mahajan (1989), Chaganti (1987), Rugman and Verbeke (1987), Wright and Parsinia (1988), McDougall and Robinson (1990), and Carter, Stearns, Reynolds and Miller (1994).

42. Examples of ways in which small businesses can create economies of scale are offered in Quinn (1992) and Ballentine, Cleveland and Koeller (1992).

43. Michael Porter's (1980) typology of competitive business strategy suggests three generic strategies: overall cost leadership, focus and differentiation.

44. See additional statistics on women-owned businesses in *The State of Small Business, 1992.*

45. See Hisrich and Brush (1986) and NFWBO (1992) for additional obstacles to start-up faced by women business owners.

46. Moore, Buttner and Rosen (1992), p. 103.

47. Hisrich and Brush (1986) and Williams, Carter and Reynolds (1993).

48. Hisrich and Brush (1986) and Williams, Carter and Reynolds (1993).

49. See Venkatraman and Prescott (1990) for full definitions of alignment and related terms.

50. Venkatraman and Camillus (1984).

51. Venkatraman and Prescott (1990), p. 1.

52. Pearce, Freeman and Robinson (1987).

53. King (1983), p. 263.

54. Schuler and Jackson (1987b), p. 139.

55. Zahra and Covin (1993), p. 470.

CHAPTER 3

Human Resource Decisions: Orientation

COMPETITIVE BUSINESS STRATEGY

Small business, as a whole, is often characterized by the relative uniqueness of its firms. Indeed, the manner in which these firms operate is as unique and idiosyncratic as the individuals running them. Strategic management captures this diversity in its contingency models.[1] Such models provide order to the uniqueness by identifying patterns in the diversity of practices. Recent work in the human resource area suggest there may be consistencies in human resource priorities across small businesses.[2]

This study relies heavily on concepts developed by the strategic management field from testing in large corporations to initiate the examination of practices in the small business. Extensive interviews with small business owners led to a continued refinement of these concepts as they are used in the small business.

One case in point is the use of the term competitive business strategy. Earlier sections of this book have detailed the disagreements between small business researchers as to the applicability of this term in small business. That controversy aside, Michael Porter's 1980 framework of competitive business strategy[3] (e.g. overall cost leadership, differentiation and focus) seems to have been largely assimilated into the working vocabulary of business in general including small businesses. Indeed, small business interviewees without exception recognized and understood the strategy concepts. However, study participants had difficulty pinpointing their firm's strategy if the differentiation category was detailed (e.g. by quality, uniqueness of product, etc.) or if the focus category was present. In the former case, participants suggested a number of the features were part of the overall firm strategy, and in the latter case, the fact that they were a small business, suggested the intent to satisfy a niche making the concept redundant.

To address these concerns, competitive business strategy was measured on a dichotomous two point scale for this project where firms pursuing a low cost orientation could be easily distinguished from those pursuing differentiation.[4]

Such a distinction in strategy makes it clear that different employee orientations are most appropriate. Further, those priorities held in each of the strategy areas differ from one another.

HUMAN RESOURCE PRIORITIES

Dyer and Holder (1988) and Schuler and Jackson (1989) have each identified a pattern of human resource decisions that respond to a firm's cost leadership or cost reduction strategy. Dyer and Holder (1988) call their human resource strategy "inducement".[5] It is characterized by programs that encourage reliable behavior in employees, where control is tight and the firm runs lean. Schuler (1989) called his philosophy "utilization"[6] in response to a firm's cost reduction strategy. Again the human resource strategy is characterized by tight control and explicit work system design.

A second human resource pattern has been identified in response to a firm's use of the differentiation business strategy. Schuler (1989) suggests firms employ an "accumulation"[7] philosophy in response to this business plan. Such a philosophy concentrates on providing employees with training to help them adapt to change, as well as using a variety of group and employee oriented practices. Dyer and Holder (1988) describe the "investment"[8] human resource strategy as one oriented to employee competence, creativity and high performance standards.

In contrast to the priorities held by firms pursuing low cost competitive strategies, those employing differentiation strategies will have business human resource strategies characterized by a long term focus, cooperative behavior, innovative tasks, job flexibility, less concern with efficiency and a results orientation; a clear distinction in priorities based upon the competitive business strategy utilized. Figure 3.1 presents the anticipated patterns in human resource priorities by competitive business strategy developed from a review of the literature in the area.

Human resource priorities reflect the general characteristics of employee behavior sought by the business owner in order to compete; in the most simplistic of terms, what the owner needs to get out of his workers. The basis of this study is a questionnaire where each priority is measured on a four point scale The scale represents a continuum with anchors placed to describe the extremes of that priority.[9] Thus, for example, the time horizon emphasized in the firm is indicated by a continuum anchored at one extreme by the statement, "My key employees must focus on the short term" and anchored at the other extreme by the statement, "My key employees must focus on the long term". Respondents are requested to indicate the point on the continuum which best represents the emphasis placed on that priority in that firm.

Overall the set of priorities represent two distinctive philosophies on the management of employees. At one extreme is a "mechanistic" view[10], represented by a short term focus, a constant, predictable approach to tasks, independent behavior, a single task focus, a concern with rules and procedures, limited personal responsibility, a major commitment to the job and a heavy focus on efficiency. In contrast, the "organic"[11] view of management represents a long term focus, creative, innovative approaches to tasks, cooperative behavior, job flexibility, a concern with outcomes, major personal responsibility, a major commitment to the organization and a minimal focus on efficiency.

A chi-square test, on an overall basis, suggests that human resource priorities are different for each competitive business strategy ($X^2 = 4.03$, $p < .05$). Specific differences in the priorities between the competitive business strategies will be examined through t-tests. Table 3.1 presents these t-test results. The t-test significance levels indicate that only half of the priorities differ based on competitive strategy. Specifically, firms pursuing a differentiation strategy are more likely to focus on a creative, innovative approach to job tasks than those firms competing on the basis of low cost. Low cost firms emphasize a more constant, predictable approach to job tasks. This finding is supported by the work of Dyer and Holder (1988). They identified a pattern of human resource decisions in response to a low cost or "inducement" strategy that emphasized reliable behavior in employees. The "investment" (or differentiation) strategy, in contrast, calls for an emphasis on creativity.[12]

Table 3.1: Human Resource Priorities by Competitive Business Strategy

	Low Cost (N=47)	Differ- entiation (N=166)	t-Value
Creative Approach	2.45	2.83	-2.13**
Commitment To Company	2.55	3.08	-2.84***
Emphasis On Efficiency	1.38	1.60	-1.80*
Emphasis On Job Outcomes	3.32	3.58	-1.72*
Personal Accountability	3.45	3.50	-0.35
Cooperative Behavior	3.26	3.37	-0.78
Emphasis On Job Flexibility	3.53	3.49	0.28
Long Term Focus	2.85	3.04	-1.19

Key: Need to approach tasks in constant, predictable manner-Need to approach tasks in a creative, innovative manner; Need to have major commitment to job itself-Need to have major commitment to company; Need to place heavy emphasis on efficiency-Need to place minimal emphasis on efficiency; Must be concerned with rules, procedures of job-Must be concerned with outcomes of job; Have limited personal accountability-Have major personal accountability; Need to focus on independent behavior-Need to focus on cooperative behavior; Must be able focus on tasks of single job-Must be able move between jobs (flexibility); Must focus on short term-Must focus on long term

*   Significant at the .10 level
**   Significant at the .05 level
***   Significant at the .01 level

The second significantly different priority between the two competitive strategies suggests that firms pursuing the differentiation strategy tend to emphasize commitment to the company while those under a low cost strategy tend to emphasize a commitment to the job. Again, this finding is supportive of the work of Dyer and Holder (1988) in their discussion of the "inducement" (low cost) versus "investment" (differentiation) strategy. In inducement, ". . . commitment is not a preoccupation, . . . [it] is instrumentally based".[13] The investment strategy, in contrast, ". . . works only if employees remain for a long time . . ."[14], suggesting a commitment to the organization.

Efficiency is the third priority that differed significantly between the two competitive strategies. However, this priority departs from the anticipated pattern of relationships between human resource priorities and competitive business strategy presented earlier. The anticipated pattern of relationships, suggests those firms pursuing a low cost strategy should demonstrate a greater focus on efficiency than their differentiation counterparts. Yet, this sample's respondents indicated just the opposite tendency.

Such a finding may be illustrative of the fact that the definitions of human resource priorities utilized in this study were derived from work which was largely descriptive in nature based upon corporate case studies. Priorities in small business may be based upon a different model. This would also suggest why past research in small business has suggested that a low cost strategy is not really a competitive option for the small firm due to an inability to create and benefit from economies of scale[15]. In short, efficiency in this study is being viewed in purely economic terms from a specialization standpoint found in many corporations. However, the definition of efficiency from a small business owner's perspective may differ and be dependent on the size of the firm or how labor intensive it is, and not the strategy of the company. The following anecdotal statement made by a small business owner during the case study phase of this research reinforces this point:

"By virtue of the fact that we are small businesses, we are niche players. That means we are always differentiating ourselves from the next small business. That differentiation may be on the basis of cost, quality, reputation, etc., but in all cases, it is differentiation. And, in all cases we must remember we are small and make the most of the niche we have carved out."

Finally, firms pursuing differentiation strategies tend to emphasize the outcome of a process in contrast to their low cost counterparts who emphasize the rules and procedures of the process itself. Schuler and Jackson (1989) suggest that ". . . priority [is given] to HRM practices that will facilitate predictable and correct role behaviors by employees . . ."[16] in a cost reduction strategy. Such practices include those activities which restrict employee discretion like ". . . fixed and explicit job descriptions that allow little room for ambiguity . . ."[17].

Since t-test results did not indicate strong support for the anticipated patterns in human resource priorities, discriminant analysis was used to determine if, given the human resource priority dimensions indicated by the respondent, one could predict or identify the competitive business strategy utilized by the firm. Table 3.2 shows the results of the discriminant analysis. 72.77% (155 of 213) of all "cases" were classified correctly as to competitive business strategy using this technique.

In total, these results suggest only limited support for the theoretical position that human resource priorities differ by competitive business strategy in small businesses. Re-examining those areas where the anticipated pattern of relationships between human resource priorities and competitive business strategies differed or were not significant in conjunction with other findings in the small business area suggests that the characteristics of competitive strategies in corporations may differ from those in small business. In short, the corporate model, while a good starting point for an analysis of small business, must be adjusted to fully understand the latter business segment.

Table 3.2: Classifying Competitive Business Strategy by Human Resource Priorities

Actual Group	Number of Cases	Predicted Group	
		1	2
Group 1 (Low Cost)	47	26	21
		55.3%	44.7%
Group 2 (Differentiation)	166	37	129
		22.3%	77.7%

For example, the finding that job flexibility, theoretically more likely to be associated with the differentiation strategy due to its focus on variety, is actually associated more often in this sample with the low cost competitive business strategy can be explained in part by a discussion held with a supermarket manager during the case study phase of this project. That manager of a family-owned supermarket had indicated that he competed on the basis of low cost. One of his staffing techniques to maintain low labor costs was to hire individuals for a range of jobs instead of just a cashier or stockboy position. As such, an individual might be serving as a cashier part of the day and then move to the bakery department during another segment of the work day. Such job flexibility was more cost effective than hiring individuals to specialize in a given position.

Further, a closer look at the issue of the owner's time horizon with regard to his firm merits discussion given the results of this survey. In 1992, 96,913 small businesses failed nationwide[18]. A 1988 *Wall Street Journal* article suggested that 60% of all entrepreneurships close within the first six years of their existence. Given these discouraging figures, it is logical that both low cost and differentiation competitors would not significantly differ with regard to their focus on the short or long term. Again, the corporate model may not fit the small business. Survival within the niche is the key focus of a small business and the time orientation associated with that function does not lend itself to the more traditional short versus long time view utilized in this survey.

GENDER

Prescriptive research has long suggested a difference between the way women approach business matters and the manner in which men deal with the same issues. Recently, some preliminary empirical research on the basis for such differences has been conducted. Chaganti (1987) looked at the ranking of a series of values by women entrepreneurs in contrast to those by male business owners. She found that women business owners possess shared values oriented toward conservatism and survival versus those of males oriented toward high growth and profit. If such basic differences exist in male and female entrepreneurs, it would follow that the human resource priorities they choose for their firms would also differ.

Rosener (1990) notes that women entrepreneurs are more likely to encourage participation, share power and information, enhance others' self-worth and get others excited about their work. Further, women business owners, like their male counterparts, have a need for independence, job satisfaction and achievement as motivations to start their businesses.[19] Finally, research indicates that women business owners tend to be more sensitive to their employees' needs than their male counterparts[20], who are more motivated by a drive to control destiny and make things happen. In fact, women cite fulfillment as the motivation for business start-up while men often indicate power and money as their motivators.[21]

Given these differences, it is likely that women business owners will tend to have human resource priorities that include a focus on the long term, creative approaches to job tasks, cooperative behavior, results orientation, minimal emphasis on efficiency and greater personal accountability. Male business owners, in contrast, will have a shorter term focus, have a predictable approach to job tasks, an independent focus on behavior, a process orientation and limited personal accountability for job duties.

Examining the t-test results in Table 3.3 indicates the groups of male and female business owners differ in their priorities only with regard to accountability and approach to tasks. Specifically, male business owners prioritize a more limited personal accountability for job duties than their female counterparts. This finding is supported by a fairly comprehensive review of gender-based studies completed by Hisrich and Brush (1986).

The studies reviewed by the pair suggest that men have a drive to control destiny. Accordingly, male business owners would limit the accountability of individual workers, allowing supervisors (presumably themselves) to have the responsibility for the job duties. Those same studies indicate that women have a need for independence. It logically follows, therefore, that such a need could translate into a priority for their workers to have major personal responsibility for job duties.

With regard to approach to tasks, some research suggests that male business owners tend to prioritize a constant, predictable approach to tasks as opposed to their female counterparts who tend to emphasize creative, innovative approaches. The National Foundation for Women Business Owners (NFWBO) recently completed a study which addresses this issue.[22] The NFWBO findings indicate that male business owners engage in "left brain" or logical thinking, while female business owners are more "right-brained" in their approaches.

Although these findings provide little support for gender-based differences in human resource priorities, they are consistent with previous results that indicate that women business owners are more similar to men across many psychological dimensions—dimensions that may shape human resource priorities.[23] A second National

Foundation for Women Business Owners study reinforced this concept, finding that women and men entrepreneurs, as a group, differ from the general working population in many psychological aspects.[24]

Table 3.3: Human Resource Priorities by Owner Gender

	Male (N=129)	Female (N=84)	t-Value
Creative Approach	2.61	2.94	-2.23**
Commitment To Company	2.91	3.05	-0.89
Emphasis On Efficiency	1.54	1.57	-0.25
Emphasis On Job Outcomes	3.54	3.49	0.48
Personal Accountability	3.40	3.62	-1.80*
Cooperative Behavior	3.28	3.45	-1.54
Emphasis on Job Flexibility	3.45	3.58	-1.21
Long Term Focus	2.93	3.11	-1.31

Key: Need to approach tasks in constant, predictable manner-Need to approach tasks in a creative, innovative manner; Need to have major commitment to job itself-Need to have major commitment to company; Need to place heavy emphasis on efficiency-Need to place minimal emphasis on efficiency; Must be concerned with rules, procedures of job-Must be concerned with outcomes of job; Have limited personal accountability-Have major personal accountability; Need to focus on independent behavior-Need to focus on cooperative behavior; Must be able focus on tasks of single job-Must be able move between jobs (flexibility); Must focus on short term-Must focus on long term

*   Significant at the .10 level
**   Significant at the .05 level
***   Significant at the .01 level

Similarly, Bowen and Hisrich (1986) found that women entrepreneurs are more masculine or instrumental in their values than women in general. In short, the incidence of business ownership and the industry in which such ownership occurs may have a greater impact on the human resource priority differences than gender does.

HUMAN RESOURCE PRIORITIES, GENDER AND STRATEGY

A more refined assessment of human resource practices in the small business can be obtained by combining gender and the competitive business strategy. This assessment allows for a more direct comparison of priorities within a chosen strategy. For example, how do the priorities of women business owners pursuing a low cost orientation differ from those male business owners with the same strategic orientation?

Table 3.4 presents the results of a t-test of human resource priorities by gender, given the competitive business strategy pursued by the owner. Within the low cost area, there are not many differences between male and female business owners. However, any differences within this area must be viewed in light of the very small number of women-owned businesses in the sample competing on the basis of this strategy.[25] Consistent with previous studies[26] women tend to concentrate their efforts in the differentiation area.

One of the significant differences between the genders within the low cost area is with regard to the emphasis placed upon job flexibility by male business owners. As indicated earlier, men tend to engage in "logical" thinking processes.[27] Further, the "corporate-based" literature examined by Dyer and Holder (1988) suggest tight control of worker activity via rigid job descriptions within the low cost area. Theoretically, job flexibility does not fit this rigid structure. Nonetheless, anecdotal information gathered during the preliminary case study phase of this research (and cited earlier) indicates job flexibility may be interpreted by the male business owner to be a way to control "his destiny".[28] The grocery store example mentioned earlier emphasizes job flexibility to limit the number of workers hired. A bake shop employee can work the cash register or stock shelves. Job flexibility in this regard limits the cost of additional personnel and is a logical response in the grocery store setting. In short, this again

Table 3.4: Human Resource Priorities by Gender Given Competitive Business Strategy

	Low Cost (N=47)		
	Male	**Female**	**t-Value**
Approach	2.52	2.29	0.80
Commitment	2.73	2.14	1.67
Efficiency	1.39	1.36	0.17
Outcomes	3.55	2.79	2.40**
Accountability	3.48	3.36	0.39
Behavior	3.27	3.21	0.21
Flexibility	3.70	3.14	1.87*
Focus	2.82	2.93	-0.35
	Differentiation (N=146)		
	Male	**Female**	**t-Value**
Approach	2.64	3.09	-2.67***
Commitment	2.96	3.23	-1.57
Efficiency	1.60	1.61	-0.11
Outcomes	3.57	3.63	-0.54
Accountability	3.38	3.67	-2.22**
Behavior	3.31	3.51	-1.71*
Flexibility	3.37	3.67	-2.46**
Focus	2.97	3.81	-1.23

Key: Need to approach tasks in constant, predictable manner-Need to approach tasks in a creative, innovative manner; Need to have major commitment to job itself-Need to have major commitment to company; Need to place heavy emphasis on efficiency-Need to place minimal emphasis on efficiency; Must be concerned with rules, procedures of job-Must be concerned with outcomes of job; Have limited personal accountability-Have major personal accountability; Need to focus on independent behavior-Need to focus on cooperative behavior; Must be able focus on tasks of single job-Must be able move between jobs (flexibility); Must focus on short term-Must focus on long term

* Significant at the .10 level
** Significant at the .05 level
*** Significant at the .01 level

suggests that the corporate model of competitive business strategy may need to be adjusted to explain findings within the small business arena. A similar argument can be made for the other significant finding in this area. Again, one would expect that a tight cost control would call for an emphasis on rules and procedures of the job. That male business owners prioritize the outcomes of the job goes against the findings of Dyer and Holder (1988) who claim that "inducers" carefully manage work systems including rules and procedures.[29] If the focus on outcomes versus rules and procedures provides for tight cost control within the small business area, then the result here is substantiated.

Within the differentiation area, there are more differences in priorities based on gender. Specifically, women business owners tend to emphasize job flexibility, independent behavior, personal accountability and creative job approaches more than their male counterparts. These findings are consistent with previous work cited in the literature.

Women entrepreneurs cite a need for independence as a motivation to start a business which may make them more likely to desire personal accountability for their own actions as well as those of their employees[30]. The emphasis that female business owners place on creative, innovative approaches to tasks corroborates earlier findings that women tend to be "right brained" thinkers in contrast to their more "logical" thinking male counterparts[31].

Rosener (1990) and Fagenson (1993) suggest that women leaders tend to encourage participation among their group members. Thus the finding here that female business owners prioritize cooperative behavior over the more individually-focused behavior favored by their male counterparts is substantiated. Finally, the finding that women emphasize job flexibility under the differentiation strategy is supported by reviews of past research conducted by Rosener (1990) and Hisrich and Brush (1986).

PRIORITIES AND FINANCIAL PERFORMANCE

Strategic management suggests that the alignment of a strategy and its context will lead to positive performance. It logically follows, therefore, that a "fit" between competitive business strategy and human resource priorities may have some impact on the financial performance of a firm. Given the stage of development of the entire concept of human resource strategy however, little empirical analysis has been done examining the impact of the human resource strategy on financial performance. Four notable exceptions are work by Nkomo (1987), Gomez-Mejia (1988), Huselid (1993) and Chaganti and Schneer (1994).

Nkomo (1987) adopted a process perspective, looking at the impact human resource planning has on organization performance. Similar to the early studies done in the strategic management area, she examined the performance of firms with formal human resource planning and those with informal or no human resource planning. 264 firms completed a questionnaire that was used to categorize companies as to type of human resource planning system (fully integrated HRP, partial HRP or no formal HRP). Traditional measures of economic performance including sales and earnings growth, and ratios of earnings to sales and earnings to total assets were also obtained. Study results showed no significant differences in performance between formal human resource planners and non-users.

In contrast, Gomez-Mejia (1988) looked at the content of human resource strategy and its impact on firm performance. The human resource management strategies of 388 Florida firms engaged in international exporting were assessed using a composite factor score. Factor scores were then used as independent variables in regression equations predicting export performance. The results indicated that the manner in which human resources are selected, deployed, compensated and motivated plays a significant part in export performance.

Huselid (1993) found that human resource management practices do influence the financial health of an organization. Using an index created by the Department of Labor, Huselid measured the sophistication of human resource practices in 968 firms. Those firms with more sophisticated human resource techniques were more profitable, had higher productivity and lower turnover than their counterparts with less sophisticated practices.

Chaganti and Schneer (1994) looked at the performance of 345 firms located in four northeastern states. They found that performance varied based on the owner-manager's mode of entry into the firm (e.g. owner started, buy-out, or family firm). Further, specific measures of performance, including sales and profitability were influenced by management actions. Rocha and Khan (1985) also found human resource decisions impact performance including sales.

Financial performance was assessed in two ways in this study. First, sample respondents self-reported their satisfaction with firm performance on a variety of financial criteria.[32] These responses were used to group firms into effective and ineffective financial performer categories. Second, indices of small business financial performance were computed by comparing the ratio of firm sales in 1993 to the number of employees. These ratios were compared to those established by the Small Business Administration[33] and, again, firms were categorized as effective and ineffective performers. The two measures were then examined for the correspondence between the two groupings.[34]

Table 3.5 presents t-test results by competitive business strategy of the differences in human resource priorities given the financial performance of the firm. The results suggest few definitive differences in priorities between the groups.

Within the low cost area, only two priorities are shown to be significantly different in t-tests between those firms labeled as effective and those ineffective financial performers. First, effective financial performers are more likely to emphasize commitment to the job. As mentioned in an earlier section of this analysis, these results find support in the work of Dyer and Holder (1988). In a low cost firm, the pair note that ". . . commitment is not a preoccupation, . . . [it] is instrumentally based".[35]

The second area shown to be significantly different is with regard to the type of behavior emphasized within the firm. T-test results suggest that effective financial performers are more likely to emphasize independent behavior by their employees. This finding is consistent with Schuler and Jackson (1987) who found that low cost firms emphasized independent behavior in their employees versus cooperative behavior in employees of a differentiation firm. These findings are also consistent with Duchesneau and Gartner (1990). In examining firms in the fresh juice distribution industry, the pair found successful companies were flexible, participative and adaptive in nature. However, this result must be examined in light of the

Table 3.5: Human Resource Priorities by Financial Effectiveness Given Competitive Business Strategy

	Low Cost		
	Effective	**Ineffective**	**t-Value**
Personal Accountability	3.41	3.63	-0.90
Creative Approach	2.33	2.68	-1.14
Cooperative Behavior	3.07	3.58	-1.98**
Commitment to Company	2.11	3.26	-4.13***
Emphasis on Efficiency	1.48	1.21	1.43
Emphasis on Job Flexibility	3.52	3.68	-0.78
Long Term Focus	2.85	2.94	-0.34
Emphasis on Job Outcomes	3.22	3.53	-1.16
	Differentiation		
	Effective	**Ineffective**	**t-Value**
Personal Accountability	3.56	3.37	1.27
Creative Approach	2.84	2.78	0.34
Cooperative Behavior	3.41	3.29	0.86
Commitment to Company	3.19	2.82	1.92*
Emphasis on Efficiency	1.57	1.69	-0.85
Emphasis on Job Flexibility	3.51	3.45	0.49
Long Term Focus	3.06	3.00	0.35
Emphasis on Job Outcomes	3.62	3.49	1.01

Key: Need to approach tasks in constant, predictable manner-Need to approach tasks in a creative, innovative manner; Need to have major commitment to job itself-Need to have major commitment to company; Need to place heavy emphasis on efficiency-Need to place minimal emphasis on efficiency; Must be concerned with rules, procedures of job-Must be concerned with outcomes of job; Have limited personal accountability-Have major personal accountability; Need to focus on independent behavior-Need to focus on cooperative behavior; Must be able focus on tasks of single job-Must be able move between jobs (flexibility); Must focus on short term-Must focus on long term

*   Significant at the .10 level
**   Significant at the .05 level
***   Significant at the .01 level

magnitude of the priority as measured. A close look at Table 3.5 indicates that while the difference between the two measures of independent behaviors in effective and ineffective performers in the low cost area may be significant, both groups are roughly in the middle of the behavior continuum, nullifying the effect.[36]

The issue of the magnitude of the priority measured also arises in the results for differentiation firms. Those labeled as effective emphasize commitment to the organization at a slightly higher and statistically significant level than their ineffective counterparts.[37]

These limited significant differences however, do not clearly indicate that human resource priorities differ on the basis of financial performance. Chaganti, Chaganti, and Mahajan (1989) note that there are few strategies associated with profitability in small businesses. Thus, if there is difficulty in labeling firms as effective and ineffective performers within given competitive business strategy groups, there will also be difficulties in examining the priorities associated with those strategies.

NOTES

1. Grant and King (1982) and Hofer and Schendel (1978) present examples of how internal and external variables fit to produce different strategies.

2. Schuler and Jackson (1989).

3. Michael Porter's *Competitive Strategy* introduces the generic strategies of overall cost leadership, differentiation and focus.

4. This dichotomous, self-report measure does, however, raise concerns as to the external validation of this item. Therefore, additional items focusing on the primary characteristics of the low cost and differentiation strategies were included. These items are based upon the work of Davis and Dess (1984) and were recommended by Dess. The correlation between the self report measure of competitive business strategy is in the acceptable range, $r = .69$, $p < .10$.

5. See Dyer and Holder (1988) for examples.

6. See Schuler (1989) for examples.

7. See Schuler (1989) for further illustrations.

8. Dyer and Holder (1988) offer examples.

9. The work of Schuler and Jackson (1989), Schuler and MacMillan (1984) and Dyer and Holder (1988) provided the basis for the development of the questionnaire's priority section. One hundred case studies in the human

resource and strategic management areas were assessed for priorities. This information combined with the information from the research in human resources, produced a listing of priorities. This list was submitted to a panel of human resource experts with an explanation as to what is meant by priorities. The panel suggested a group of priorities which were incorporated into a priority scale. This scale was examined by a small group of business owners for clarity. Their comments led to the refinement of the priority scale to the eight items included in this questionnaire. A pre-test of the questionnaire indicated an alpha coefficient of .77 for the scale.

10. See Burns and Stalker (1961) for a detailed description of how the theory was developed. Taylor (1911) serves as the basis for the later writing.

11. Burns and Stalker (1961) provide the theory for this label.

12. Dyer and Holder (1988) offer examples. See Schuler and Jackson (1989) and Schuler and MacMillan (1984) for additional examples.

13. Dyer and Holder (1988), p. 1-22.

14. Dyer and Holder (1988), p. 1-25.

15. A host of researchers make this argument including Miller and Toulouse (1986), Chaganti, Chaganti and Mahajan (1989), Chaganti (1987), Rugman and Verbeke (1987), Wright and Parsinia (1988), McDougall and Robinson (1990), and Carter, Stearns, Reynolds and Miller (1994).

16. Schuler and Jackson (1989), p. 90.

17. Schuler (1987), p. 213.

18. According to statistics in *The State of Small Business, 1992*.

19. Hisrich and Brush (1986) provide a thorough assessment of key differences in male and female business owners.

20. Brush (1992) updated research on gender-based differences in psychological characteristics of business owners.

21. Brush (1995) provides an extensive discussion of motivations for business start-up in women.

22. See National Foundation for Women Business Owners (1994) for further distinctions in male versus female business owners.

23. Brush (1995).

24. The National Foundation for Women Business Owners (1994) study details differences between business owners and the general working population.

25. Only 14 of the women-owned businesses in this study indicated a low cost strategy as their main orientation.

26. See Williams, Carter and Reynolds (1993) for a detailed examination of industry participation and strategic orientation by male and female business owners.

27. NFWBO (1994).

28. Hisrich and Brush (1986).

29. See Dyer and Holder (1988) for a discussion of such rules and procedures.

30. Hisrich and Brush (1986).

31. NFWBO (1994) and *Newsweek* (1995) present complementary findings. These findings are especially interesting since they reach similar conclusions, but the NFWBO report is psychologically-based and used focus groups; while the *Newsweek* piece is biologically-based using clinical material.

32. The self-report measure of firm performance was chosen for this study for a variety of reasons. First, small firms, such as those which are the focus of this study, tend to be very reluctant to release any objective material related to the performance of their firms. Further, since many of the small firms are private, public performance data, from which to check the accuracy of any information given, is largely unavailable.

A study by Dess and Robinson (1984) indicates that self-report data and actual performance are correlated. Although that study in no way suggested self-report data should be gathered instead of objective material, it did lend credibility to those situations in which "hard" data is unavailable. In addition, Brush and VanderWerf (1990) conducted a meta-analysis of recent literature using subjective responses in evaluating performance. They found that such single respondent measures of performance were valid. They note, "Subjective measures proved a very consistent measure of performance information and did not vary widely in accuracy from objective measures." (p.2).

The measure of firm performance used in this questionnaire varies from that used by Covin and Slevin (1986, 1988a, and 1988b) in that it is not weighted by an importance factor to create a performance index. Given the dearth of performance data in the small business area (Brush, 1990), there is no a priori justification for suggesting that any of these financial measures is more important than any other or that small business owners view them as such. The levels of satisfaction were summed across all financial criteria. Firms whose total was between 5 and 15 were classified as ineffective performers and those with totals of 16 or more were classified as effective performers. Potential issues of external validation of such a self-report measure were addressed by requesting additional information from the business owners. Specifically, the questionnaire asks for the previous three years' sales (billings) figures and the number of employees employed by the firm. Sixty nine percent of the firms responding to the questionnaire completed these items.

33. Ratios of sales to number of employees were calculated using the last year's sales figures. These ratios were compared to those established by the Small Business Administration (SBA Handbook, 1994) as standards for each industry. Firms were classified as ineffective performers if they fell short of the industry ratio by more than 20%. All others were classified as effective performers. This objective measure corresponded with the self-report measures at a satisfactory level ($r = .61$, $p < .10$)

34. The correspondence between the two measures of performance is $r = .61$, $p < .10$.

35. Dyer and Holder (1988), p. 1-22.

36. The mean of effective financial performers was 3.07. The mean of ineffective financial performers was 3.58.

37. The mean of effective performers was 3.19, that of ineffective performers, 2.82.

CHAPTER 4

Human Resource Decisions: Practices

HUMAN RESOURCE PROGRAMMING AND STRATEGY

The proposition that a chosen competitive business strategy makes different employee orientations or human resource priorities most appropriate, also suggests that differing human resource programs or practices will evoke the desired behaviors. Simply put, human resource programs in firms with low cost competitive strategies differ from those in firms pursuing a differentiation strategy.

Work by Dyer and Holder (1988) and Schuler and Jackson (1989) has examined some of the programming activities utilized by firms employing each competitive strategy. Firms choosing a low cost competitive business strategy used human resource programs that included explicit job descriptions with rigid job grades, individual piece rate systems and pay for performance systems based on clearly defined short term goals.

Firms pursuing a differentiation competitive business strategy, on the other hand, had human resource programs that included employee training and development activities, job rotation, and open communication systems.

Fombrun and Wally (1989) also examined such human resource programming activities in relationship to the competitive strategy chosen by a firm. Ninety five small businesses which had experienced a five year surge in growth were analyzed for the fit between strategy and structure (defined as strategy and cultural, staffing and development and appraisal and reward practices).

Firms pursuing the low cost strategy were less likely to use participative decision making, tended to utilize promotion from within policies and formalized their employee evaluation process. Firms employing a quality strategy, on the other hand, also tended to promote from within, encouraged human resource planning, and tended to utilize an incentive system. Schneider and Bowen (1993) also documented the importance of human resource practices to the delivery of quality service (the competitive business strategy) in a group of firms operating in the banking industry.

To date, the relationship between human resource programming and the choice of competitive business strategy has been investigated in the literature in a largely descriptive, and occasionally, prescriptive manner. What limited empirical analysis has been completed, focuses on the relationship between a specific human resource function (i.e. compensation and competitive business strategy). This study tries to broaden the analysis by assessing the entire spectrum of human resource functions and its relationship to the choice of competitive business strategy. This research project attempts to comprehensively examine human resource practices in the small business, by first, investigating each programmatic element separately and then assessing them as an overall integrated programmatic element.

Human resource practices, for this study, were assessed via responses to questionnaires completed by owner-managers in each participating small business. Questionnaire items were created following substantial review of pertinent literature[1], and numerous rounds of pre-testing with a separate sample of small business owners whose characteristics match that of the target sample. Programs, plans, and policies were assessed in the compensation, staffing, training and development, performance appraisal and employee relations areas. Respondents are asked to indicate the importance of these programs to the firm or their frequency of use in the firm.

Tables 4.1 through 4.5 present t-test results of human resource programming by competitive business strategy. Each functional human resource area is examined individually. An overall programmatic assessment is also presented.

Compensation

In the compensation area (Table 4.1), for example, half of the programmatic elements examined in this study differ based on the competitive business strategy utilized by the firm. Specifically, results indicate that in firms pursuing a differentiation strategy, individual employee contributions to the firm play a role in pay decisions, pay is based on individual and group achievements, employee pay is secret, and the focus is long term. In differentiation firms, pay is based on the mastery of job skills while in low cost firms, job-based pay is the focus.

Balkin and Gomez-Mejia examined the differences in compensation program elements between manufacturing firms pursuing a growth strategy versus those pursuing a maintenance strategy. The pair found that firms pursuing a growth strategy emphasized incentives in their compensation package to a greater degree than their counterparts pursuing a maintenance strategy. Thus, this study's finding that individual and group achievements impact pay is supported.[2] Further, Buller, Beck-Dudley, and McEvoy (1989) found that law firms pursuing a low cost strategy used fewer incentives in their compensation packages than those law firms pursuing a differentiation strategy. Jackson, Schuler and Rivero (1989) also found incentives, such as bonuses, were used in firms pursuing a differentiation strategy through innovation.

The second compensation element that clearly differs based upon the choice of competitive business strategy is whether pay is based upon job placement in a pay structure (job-based pay) versus mastery of job skills (skill-based pay). Milkovich and Boudreau (1994) note that skill based systems increase the breadth of employee skills.[3] Employees with a wider range of skills and thus greater potential job assignment flexibility are desirable in a firm pursuing differentiation.[4] This study's sample clearly reflects the use of skill-based pay systems in differentiation firms and job-based systems in low cost firms.

The final compensation program element significantly different based upon the type of competitive business strategy pursued, relates to the firm's policy with regard to pay secrecy. As the t-test results of Table 4.1 suggest, firms pursuing differentiation were significantly more likely to utilize a policy of pay secrecy than their low cost counterparts. A review of relevant compensation literature offers very little guidance for whether this finding is consistent with past studies' results. However, it could make sense if some objective job evaluation

Table 4.1: Compensation Programs by Competitive Business Strategy

	Low Cost	Differentiation	t-Value
Contributions to firm impact pay	3.70	4.06	-1.91*
Rates above competitors	3.47	3.56	-0.50
Rates below competitors	2.53	2.25	1.58
Pay based on individual achievement	3.40	3.92	-2.49**
Job-based pay	3.73	3.05	3.24***
Non-monetary rewards	2.70	2.95	-1.27
Long term focus rewarded	3.44	3.77	-1.85*
Pay based on group achievements	2.84	3.28	-2.42**
Pay information secret in firm	3.79	4.23	-2.13**
Short term focus rewarded	2.91	2.98	-0.36
Skill based pay	3.42	3.78	-1.68*
Seniority impacts pay	3.11	3.08	-0.16
Pay rates set by comparison to external market	3.00	2.73	1.43
Pay rates set by job comparison within firm	3.07	2.83	1.06

*   Significant at the .10 level
**   Significant at the .05 level
***   Significant at the .01 level

method were utilized (such as point or classification) in the low cost firm. In contrast, in the differentiation firm, special negotiation may take place for contract development, a much more secretive method. As Gomez-Mejia and Balkin (1992) note in an analysis of past research on elements of compensation strategies, the issue of pay secrecy has not been widely examined in the past, particularly with regard to its utilization under a given competitive business strategy.

Staffing

Table 4.2 presents t-test results of the differences in the type of staffing programs used given the competitive business strategy pursued. Once again, the results provide little support for the proposition that differences do occur based on the strategy pursued.

A great deal of prescriptive work supports the idea of matching strategy to the overall staffing programs used by a firm. Olian and Rynes (1984), for example, describe the specific selection criteria, recruitment method choice, method of marketing the position to a prospective candidate, and selection device that best addresses the needs of the strategies in the Miles and Snow (1978) typology.[5] Others,[6] present a normative description of the link between a specific part of the selection program (assessment of individual characteristics) and the business strategy pursued by the firm.

Most empirical work in this area has examined an aspect of the selection program and its relationship to the competitive business strategy[7]. Gupta and Govindarajan (1984), examined the match between specific characteristics of general managers in 58 diversified firms and the effectiveness with which specific competitive business strategies were implemented. The findings suggest that careful attention to the selection devices used to ascertain managerial characteristics can benefit a firm. Buller, Beck-Dudley and McEvoy (1989) got similar results from their study of law firms. Specifically, the trio found that firms pursuing a differentiation strategy shaped their selection criteria to assess experience and ability, while those utilizing a low cost strategy looked for ability alone.

Table 4.2: Staffing Programs by Competitive Business Strategy

	Low cost	Differ-entiation	t-Value
Ability tests	2.64	2.67	-0.13
Biographical Information	4.34	4.41	-0.38
Personality tests	1.55	1.98	-2.40**
Interviews	4.77	4.89	-0.93
Honesty tests	1.32	1.59	-2.41**
Performance Tests	2.49	2.81	-1.29
References	4.09	4.38	-1.44
Public agencies	2.21	2.31	-0.55
Private agencies	1.85	2.10	-1.32
Personal referrals	3.48	3.90	-2.37**
Newspapers	3.36	3.27	0.44
Job fairs	1.13	1.34	-2.76***
Electronic bulletin boards	1.00	1.22	-4.11***
Networking	2.47	2.97	-2.13**
Walk-ins	2.77	3.10	-1.95**
Written job descriptions on file	2.72	3.13	-1.66*
Job duties shaped by employees	3.17	3.22	-0.23
Skills kept on file	2.38	2.82	-2.07**
Firm forecasts numbers needed	2.93	3.09	-0.79
No guaranteed employment	3.68	3.79	-0.42
Promotion from within policy	2.86	3.02	-0.75
Hire those with narrow skill range	2.09	2.10	-0.08
Informal testing used in selection	2.58	2.56	0.04
Hire based on match skills and job	4.40	4.14	1.53
Hire based on fit	3.68	3.87	-1.31
Hire based on potential	3.78	3.79	-0.04

*   Significant at the .10 level
**   Significant at the .05 level
*** Significant at the .01 level

Specific staffing elements utilized with either competitive business strategy are discussed only in general terms in the largely prescriptive work done to date in the area. Anecdotal information from the interviews conducting in phase one of this study were examined for possible suggestions.

A crane owner pursuing the low cost competitive business strategy noted:

> "I use the same [recruiting] sources I always do, hiring through newspapers, but mostly referrals. I've always got what I wanted in the past, so I'll keep at it. Since I run lean and mean, I can't shop around for other sources."

Similarly, the low cost firms would be interested in using the minimum number of selection devices that deliver individuals with desired skills. A machine shop operator pursing low cost as a strategy describes this practice:

> "How do I make my decisions? I chat with 'em to find out how much they know about what we do here. Then, they show me by working the machines. I look for current good skills. If I get 'em, I get less waste. That's my aim."

The results of this study suggest slight differences in recruiting sources and selection tools based upon the competitive business strategy chosen. Specifically, firms pursuing differentiation tend to use the candidate recruiting sources of electronic bulletin boards, job fairs, personal referrals and walk-ins more than their low cost counterparts. The number and range of sources affords the differentiation firm a greater opportunity to secure candidates with the diversity of skills necessary to compete under that strategy[8]. Further, employing multiple sources would not address the tight cost considerations of the crane operator noted above. Differentiation firms also distinguish themselves from their low cost counterparts by using personality and honesty tests as selection devices.

Again, anecdotal information from the interview phase supports the finding. A computer software development firm owner noted:

> "I give prospective candidates as many tests as I can—you know, honesty, personality, ability (like mental, motor coordination) and anything else I can find. I expect my employees to grow in producing the software. This is a creative business. There are no standards to abide by. We set 'em—tomorrow we could write the next blockbuster program, therefore I need to really know what my crew's future is all about—including their potential. So, I get a lot."

Training and Development

Table 4.3 presents the results of a t-test on differences in training and development programs based on the type of competitive business strategy employed by the firm. Once more the results selectively support this proposition. Differences in training and development programming between the firms in this sample are concentrated in the types of training methods utilized. Firms pursuing a differentiation strategy utilize computer-aided instruction, lectures and presentations, videotapes and role playing more than their low cost counterparts. In addition, differentiation firms tend to focus their training efforts on the development of firm-specific and group dynamics skills.

These findings indicate that differentiation firms in this sample are utilizing a wide variety of training methods. However, these methods are designed to make the process of training and development efficient in its administration. That is, employees may be trained on any topic when it best fits their work schedules, just by watching a videotape or completing a computer-aided instruction segment. Given the earlier discussion, one might assume that such efficiency would be better suited to low cost firms. However, study interviews indicated that low cost firms perform no more training and development than that mandated by law or required for equipment utilization.

Table 4.3: Training and Development by Competitive Business Strategy

	Low cost	Differ-entiation	t-Value
Training to improve performance	3.91	4.03	-0.60
Training to teach future skills	3.13	3.48	-1.62
Training to enhance promotability	3.25	3.28	-0.12
Training in government mandated areas	1.95	2.01	-0.22
All employees eligible	4.22	3.94	1.58
Training regularly scheduled	2.76	3.08	-1.49
Lectures	2.62	3.31	-3.15***
Videotapes	2.49	2.96	-2.33**
Computer-aided instruction	1.87	2.45	-3.01***
Role playing	1.57	2.46	-4.68***
On the job training	4.47	4.37	0.65
Basic writing skills	2.17	2.44	-1.28
Oral communication skills	2.63	2.98	-1.69*
Decision making skills	2.59	2.95	-1.65*
Basic production skills	3.30	3.10	0.79
Quality skills	3.26	3.35	-0.38
Group dynamics skills	1.98	2.43	-2.27**
OSHA required training	2.89	2.72	0.68

*   Significant at the .10 level
**   Significant at the .05 level
*** Significant at the .01 level

The oft-cited grocery store owner notes:

"I train only in required OSHA areas. Some guys now have consultants run motivation clinics to help their employees be happy, even to the customer. Right! I told you before that a monkey could do some of these. What would be the point of all that training?"

In short, many of the low cost firms in this sample do not provide training for their employees beyond that which is required by government mandate. Accordingly, issues of efficiency in such training are also of little concern.

As Deshpande and Golhar (1994) note, work focusing on training and development in small businesses has been largely prescriptive or process in nature. The limited empirical work done provides little support for this study's findings. For example, Buller, Beck-Dudley and McEvoy (1989), in their study of law firms, found that those employing a low cost strategy had minimal training and development programming available to their employees. Differentiation firms, in contrast, support training and development. However, the degree of that support as well as the kind of support given were not examined in the study.

Jackson, Schuler and Rivero (1989) examined the types of training available to both hourly and managerial employees in firms using an innovation strategy. They found that hourly employees were offered more total hours and received more training related to skills needed currently and in the future than the average employee. Managerial employees received more training emphasizing promotion, transfer and future company needs than the average employee. Though these issues were examined in the current study, no differences were found in the sample of small businesses investigated.

Performance Appraisal

Table 4.4 presents t-test results of performance appraisal programming given the competitive business strategy employed by the firm. In general, differentiation firms make multiple uses of their performance results and gather them in differing ways from their low cost counterparts.

Specifically, differentiation firms are more likely to have formal written evaluation systems that utilize the job incumbent as an evaluator than the low cost firms. Further, differentiation firms are more likely to use performance appraisal results to make decisions with regard to training and development and performance improvement than their low cost counterparts.

Such a finding re-emphasizes a common thread in the low cost firms. That is, very little attention is focused on training and development beyond that required by law. Therefore, there is little need for performance appraisals to be formally developed to address training and development needs. The only evaluation information necessary is that likely to be utilized by the firm, in short, a limited amount with the low cost firm.

Buller, Beck-Dudley and McEvoy (1989) found similar practices in their law firm sample. Law firms pursuing differentiation were more likely to have formal performance evaluation systems that assessed employee quality than their low cost counterparts. Although relatively little empirical work[9] has been done in the performance appraisal programming area, this study's findings are in line with other existing results.

Table 4.4: Performance Appraisal Programs by Competitive Business Strategy

	Low Cost	Differ-entiation	t -Value
Firm has formal written procedure	2.52	3.38	-2.85***
Results used for compensation	3.29	3.56	-1.29
Results used for training	2.97	3.35	-1.74*
Results used for performance imp.	3.37	3.87	-2.26**
Results used for staffing	3.03	3.20	-0.74
Evaluations regularly scheduled	3.23	3.55	-1.27
Evaluation as a team	2.73	2.77	-0.17
Evaluation by specific standards	3.63	3.57	0.30
Employees help determine standards	2.68	3.03	-1.65*
Self evaluation	1.57	2.75	-6.33***
Supervisors evaluate	3.87	4.05	-0.83
Customers evaluate	2.47	2.74	-1.12

*   Significant at the .10 level
**   Significant at the .05 level
*** Significant at the .01 level

Employee Relations

Table 4.5 presents the t-test results of employee relations programming utilized by firms employing differing competitive business strategies. These results offer new insights into the small business area as no previous work has examined such programming in this manner. In this study, firms pursuing differentiation are more likely to use different methods in communicating with their employees than firms pursuing a low cost strategy. Specifically, differentiation firms use employee handbooks, memos, newsletters and suggestion systems more often than do low cost firms. Again no small business studies to date have provided findings which either corroborate or dissent from these results. Miles and Snow (1984) suggest that a prospector firm (similar to the differentiation firm of this study) seeks to enhance participation to increase employee involvement. One such method of increasing participation is through enhanced two-way communication. The larger number of communication methods employed by the differentiation firms of this study suggest that such a method is being employed by small business firms.

Overall Programmatic Findings

While on an individual function basis the results provide limited support for the hypothesized relationship, it is important to examine these same results across functions to detect possible patterns in the programming. A simple assessment, devised by the researcher, was utilized in this study. All human resource programming elements, with statistically significant differences between the low cost and differentiation strategies, were assessed as to whether the element represented a procedure (i.e., how the human resource decision is made) versus a policy (i.e., what the human resource decision is), whether the element as assessed is oriented toward the group or individual, and whether it is firm specific or more general in nature. While this assessment is rudimentary at best, it does represent a means to discerning a human resource profile unique to the given competitive strategy. Appendix 4 presents the definitions utilized in this assessment as well as justification for the labeling of each programmatic element. Figure 4.1 presents the labels for each programmatic element.

Table 4.5: Employee Relations Programs by Competitive Business Strategy

	Low cost	Differ- entiation	t- Value
Employee handbooks	2.64	3.09	-1.81*
Newsletters	1.53	2.16	-3.81***
Direct home mailings	1.40	1.47	-0.46
Internal memos	3.00	3.48	-2.13**
Meetings	3.98	4.16	-1.16
Bulletin board postings	2.91	3.15	-1.11
Suggestion systems	2.60	2.99	-1.86*
Open door policy	4.04	4.31	-1.57
Worker-management committee	2.45	2.71	-1.19
Multiple step with outside arbitration	1.53	1.51	0.11
Multiple step with owner decision	3.29	3.23	0.23
One step with owner decision	2.40	2.38	0.07

* Significant at the .10 level
** Significant at the .05 level
*** Significant at the .01 level

As Figure 4.1indicates, in the differentiation firms, overall programming elements are procedural in nature. The significant elements are group oriented and largely firm specific. A similar assessment of a pattern of human resource programming in the low cost firm is problematic given the results from this sample. A closer look at Tables 4.1-4.5 indicates that the level at which a particular element is present in the firm is very similar for both low cost and differentiation firms. Only in the low cost firms' usage of job-based pay versus the skill-based pay of the differentiation firms is a distinction clear. This suggests that these human resource programming elements are present in small businesses as a whole regardless of competitive strategy chosen. Any distinction between the two competitive strategy profiles would likely be the focus of a particular programming element, and not its mere presence. This study was not designed to make such a distinction.

However, interview data does suggest this may be an option (program focus not program presence) by which future programmatic profiles may be distinguished. The grocer, who utilizes a low cost strategy, in a second conversation on training, notes:

"I train my people according to OSHA-required regs [regulations] for slicers, compactors, etc. Beyond that, I don't train. I teach them how to use a cash register or do their job during orientation. Do we have seminars in improving customer relations—no way. It's too expensive for what you get from it."

Compare this quotation to that of the computer software firm owner cited in the staffing section of this chapter. As per the questionnaire of this study, both would indicate the presence of a training program. The focus of that program however would not be clear without a verbal description as to its orientation.

PROGRAMMING AND GENDER

Again, demographic influences like gender, can be examined for their impact on a firm's human resource programming. The obvious assumption is that programming differs based upon the gender of the owner. Rosener (1990) noted an interactive approach works for women to involve, communicate and reward employees versus the traditional "command and control" method used by men. Her work further suggests that women business owners may be more prone to using team-based performance appraisal as well as more group oriented compensation practices. Further, multi-skill training and development programs would be instituted. Staffing activities would involve employees in decision making such as in the shaping of job duties. Finally, employee relations programs would have a heavy employee involvement orientation.

The trend toward increasing numbers of women in the entrepreneurial field has led researchers to begin to examine whether gender is an issue with regard to any of the start-up, development or on-going management activities involved in a small business. As Brush (1994) notes, little empirical evidence can be found in the literature to substantiate the current assumptions guiding our research: "... that women-owned businesses are the same as men-owned firms, that theories developed from studies of men and their businesses apply to women and their businesses ...".[10].

Rosener's (1990) work also suggests that women business owners may be more prone to using team based performance appraisal as well as more group oriented compensation practices. Further, multi-skill training and development programs would be instituted. Staffing activities would involve employees in decision making such as in the shaping of job duties. Finally, employee relations programs would have a heavy employee involvement orientation. This study seeks to add to the empirical database testing such assumptions by examining each programmatic activity and then assessing them together as an integrated overall approach to human resource management. Tables 4.6 through 4.10 present the results of t-tests examining human resource programming based upon the gender of the business owner. In general, the types of human resource programming utilized by women in their firms do differ from that used by male business owners.

Compensation

Table 4.6 presents the results of compensation programming as it differs based upon the business owner's gender. Specifically, male business owners are more likely to create compensation programs which emphasize contributions to the firm and seniority in making pay decisions, base pay rates on comparing similar jobs within the firm, and utilize a job-based pay system. Female business owners, on the other hand, are more likely to emphasize non-monetary rewards in their firms.

Support for the use of job-based pay systems in male-owned businesses can be found in the work of Williams, Carter, and Reynolds (1993). Firms pursuing low cost strategies are predominately owned by males. Since job-based pay systems are characteristic of firms pursuing cost efficiencies [11], the gender based results indicated in the table are likely.

The use of seniority as an element in compensation programming is also supported in the literature. Males tend to predominate in manufacturing industries[12] where seniority is a frequently utilized element of human resource programming. Further, most entrepreneurs tend to use their past experience and education as the basis for development of their businesses[13]. It is likely then, that the use of seniority and a system that compares jobs within a firm could be the result of male business owners' experiences, experiences females, by and large, do not share.

Table 4.6: Compensation Programs by Gender of Owner

	Male (n=129)	Female (n=84)	t-Value
Contributions to firm impact pay	4.10	3.79	2.04**
Rates above competitors'	3.57	3.48	0.55
Rates below competitors'	2.35	2.26	0.51
Pay based on individual achievement	3.80	3.80	0.00
Job-based pay	3.43	2.81	3.37**
Non-monetary rewards	2.62	3.30	-4.12**
Long term focus rewarded	3.76	3.61	1.02
Pay based on group achievements	3.16	3.23	-0.45
Pay information secret in firm	4.23	3.98	1.51
Short term focus rewarded	2.89	3.09	-1.16
Skill based pay	3.73	3.65	0.47
Seniority impacts pay	3.27	2.80	2.72**
Pay rates set by comparison external market	2.86	2.69	0.96
Pay rates set by job comparison within firm	3.11	2.49	3.32**

*   Significant at the .10 level
**   Significant at the .05 level
*** Significant at the .01 level

Gilligan (1982) and Powell (1988) note that males exhibit personality and psychological characteristics that could be described as "competitive". That competitive nature could lead to the use of reward systems based on recognized "contributions" from that competition.

Finally, that female business owners are more likely to utilize non-monetary pay systems than their male counterparts also finds support in the literature. At start-up, women have less capital for investment relative to men[14]. Therefore, they have less money with which to reward employees and must explore other avenues to motivate their workers. Further, women tend to lack financial skills as per their male counterparts[15] and thus turn to other areas to reward their employees.

Staffing

Table 4.7 presents the significant t-test results of staffing programs by the gender of the business owner. Elements of the staffing programs differ between the genders based upon the policies established, recruiting sources utilized and staffing tools employed.

Male business owners are more likely than female business owners to utilize the recruiting services of agencies, both public and private. With regard to women-business owners, they are more likely to utilize networks in recruiting than their male counterparts. Rosener (1990) and Rosener, McAllister and Stephens, (1990) support this finding by noting the use by women of "web-like" communication structures versus the more traditional top-down, command and control approach of men.

Male business owners tend to use the interview and informal testing as selection tools while women business owners use interviews and personality testing. Since this sample finds males heavily concentrated in the low cost competitive strategy area, and informal testing is a technique that produces cost efficiencies, it is not surprising to find that males use it in their businesses more than females do. Although statistically there is a significant difference between the use of the interview by men and women business owners, the magnitude of the score for each gender indicates it is widely used by both.

Table 4.7: Staffing Programs by Owner Gender

	Male	Female	t-Value
Ability tests	2.63	2.71	-0.42
Biographical Information	4.43	4.33	0.66
Personality tests	1.67	2.20	-2.83***
Interviews	4.95	4.73	2.16**
Honesty tests	1.50	1.60	-0.69
Performance Tests	2.67	2.85	-0.81
References	4.31	4.31	-0.02
Public agencies	2.43	2.06	2.30**
Private agencies	2.15	1.88	1.66*
Personal referrals	3.80	3.81	-0.03
Newspapers	3.29	3.27	0.11
Job fairs	1.27	1.33	-0.67
Electronic bulletin boards	1.20	1.13	0.89
Networking	2.65	3.18	-2.53***
Walk-ins	3.05	2.98	0.49
Written job descriptions on file	2.77	3.48	-3.42***
Job duties shaped by employees	3.20	3.23	-0.14
Skills kept on file	2.66	2.83	-0.94
Firm forecasts numbers needed	3.01	3.12	-0.62
No guaranteed employment	3.81	3.69	0.62
Promotion from within policy	2.99	2.97	0.10
Hire those with narrow skill range	2.13	2.05	0.51
Informal testing used in selection	2.71	2.35	1.72*
Hire based on match skills and job	4.21	4.19	0.14
Hire based on fit	3.70	4.02	-2.57***
Hire based on potential	3.89	3.63	1.92*

*   Significant at the .10 level
**   Significant at the .05 level
***   Significant at the .01 level

Women business owners tend to adopt a policy of assessing the "fit" between the person and the organization in making a selection decision and to utilize written job descriptions in their firms. This idea of matching an individual to his work is a normal extension of the socialization of women since girls are largely taught to define themselves in terms of others[16]. This leads to a definition of self in the role of nurturer—a role which makes certain all is right with the workers[17].

The presence of written job descriptions being kept on file in women-owned businesses is another example of the socialization of women. In this case, attention to detail is the duty of the role. The family business literature widely notes the "invisible" role [18] women play, particularly in the family-owned firm. Women generally play a "behind the scenes" role in family business, carrying out bookkeeping and clerical duties, such as keeping the job descriptions on file.

Training and Development

Table 4.8 shows the types of training programs used by male and female business owners. Programming differences based upon gender are clearly evident with regard to the numbers and types of training policies, methods and skill areas addressed by the business owners and uses of the training outcomes. Specifically, women business owners offer their employees a far greater number of training and development programs with greater variety than do their male counterparts.

Female business owners have a policy of holding regularly scheduled training sessions and using those sessions to improve performance, enhance promotability and develop future skills. They also offer programming in decision making and group dynamics and utilize on-the-job training and role playing methods that their male counterparts do not. Male business owners, in contrast, offer basic production and OSHA-mandated training more than their female counterparts.

Specific human resource programming that differs on the basis of gender has not been detailed to this point in the literature. However, general support for these findings can be found if the overall pattern in training and development programming is examined. Male business owners offer programming generally associated with a manufacturing setting. As noted earlier, men tend to predominate in manufacturing firms and take their experiences with them to a new venture[19]. Accordingly, basic production skill development as well as OSHA-mandated training would be "male-based" activities. Women business owners, concentrated in the service sector, and socialized to be nurturers[20], offer programming that enhances individuals' abilities in a variety of areas.

Table 4.8: Training and Development Programs by Owner Gender

	Male	Female	t-Value
Training to improve performance	3.86	4.23	-2.48***
Training to teach future skills	3.18	3.76	-3.31***
Training to enhance promotability	3.11	3.51	-2.10**
Training in government mandated areas	2.10	1.82	1.48
All employees eligible	3.98	4.02	-0.23
Training regularly scheduled	2.79	3.34	-2.76***
Lectures	3.06	3.30	-1.17
Videotapes	2.74	3.04	-1.41
Computer-aided instruction	2.11	2.65	-2.95***
Role playing	1.94	2.77	-3.97***
On the job training	4.26	4.59	-2.32**
Basic writing skills	2.29	2.51	-1.12
Oral communication skills	2.71	3.22	-2.57***
Decision making skills	2.71	3.13	-2.28**
Basic production skills	3.32	2.88	2.25**
Quality skills	3.37	3.27	0.54
Group dynamics skills	2.17	2.59	-2.33**
OSHA required training	3.00	2.37	3.07***

*   Significant at the .10 level
**   Significant at the .05 level
***   Significant at the .01 level

Performance Appraisal

Table 4.9 features the t-test results of performance appraisal programming by business owner's gender. Women business owners differ from male business owners with regard to their performance evaluation policies, who participates in the evaluation session itself and how performance results are used. Female entrepreneurs in this sample are more likely to hold regularly scheduled performance appraisals that utilize a formal written procedure focusing on specific standards. Employees are more likely to have helped determine the standards on which they are appraised and to evaluate themselves than in a male-owned firm. Finally, women business owners are more likely to utilize the information from the appraisals in training and development programming.

The results of Tables 4.9 and 4.10 are supportive of the work of Kohlberg (1981) and Gilligan (1982) who suggest that women define themselves in terms of their relationships toward others. This leads to a female "role" of nurturer[21]. From this study's perspective, the female business owner "nurtures" her employees by offering the opportunity to develop their "human capital" through performance assessment and training and development programming.

Employee Relations

Table 4.10 concludes the gender based assessment of human resource programming by looking at differences between men and women business owners in their employee relations programs. The only significant difference between the groups is the male business owners' more likely usage of a multiple step grievance resolution procedure that ends with an outside arbitrator. Since no previous work has examined gender based differences in these types of human resource programming, it is unclear whether this study's findings are representative of other small businesses.

Table 4.9: Performance Appraisal Programs by Owner Gender

	Male (n=129)	Female (n=84)	Female (n=84)
Firm has formal written procedure	2.99	3.52	-2.16**
Results used for compensation	3.44	3.61	-0.93
Results used for training	3.01	3.68	-3.74***
Results used for performance imp.	3.70	3.85	-0.79
Results used for staffing	3.17	3.14	0.18
Evaluations regularly scheduled	3.16	3.97	-4.36***
Evaluation as a team	2.73	2.81	-0.46
Evaluation by specific standards	3.43	3.82	-2.44**
Employees help determine standards	2.79	3.20	-2.12**
Self evaluation	2.15	3.04	-4.18***
Supervisors evaluate	4.00	4.04	-0.22
Customers evaluate	2.60	2.81	-0.92

*   Significant at the .10 level
**   Significant at the .05 level
***   Significant at the .01 level

Overall Programmatic Assessment

Though specific human resource functions suggest few gender based differences, when considered in the aggregate, differences in human resource programming are clearly evident in this sample. In general, human resource programming of male business owners seems to be "firm specific" in its nature. That is, the orientation of programming seems to be one of immediate use in the firm. Female business owners' programming, in contrast, seems to be directed to the development of the individual employee in a larger, human capital sense, with skills useful in firms beyond that currently employing the individual.

PROGRAMMING, GENDER AND STRATEGY

Tables 4.11 through 4.15 present results within a given competitive strategy of the different human resource programming utilized by male and female business owners. In general, the there is only limited evidence that the program differs given the owner's gender. However, there are some emerging patterns among the programs utilized which suggest the need for further investigation in this area.

Table 4.10: Employee Relations Programs by Owner Gender

	Male (n=129)	Female (n=84)	t-Value
Employee handbooks	3.07	2.87	0.96
Newsletters	1.99	2.07	-0.43
Direct home mailings	1.50	1.39	0.99
Internal memos	3.39	3.34	0.25
Meetings	4.08	4.18	-0.78
Bulletin board postings	3.21	2.92	1.58
Suggestion systems	2.81	3.05	-1.31
Open door policy	4.24	4.27	-0.17
Worker-management committee	2.55	2.82	-1.23
Multiple step with outside arbitration	1.63	1.34	2.00**
Multiple step with owner decision	3.10	3.46	-1.63
One step with owner decision	2.45	2.26	0.92

*   Significant at the .10 level
**   Significant at the .05 level
*** Significant at the .01 level

Compensation

Table 4.11 presents the types of compensation programming utilized within low cost or differentiation firms that differ based upon the gender of the company's owner. However, as mentioned in earlier sections of this analysis, all comments regarding female businesses pursuing the low cost strategy must be prefaced by the fact that such results are based upon a sample of fourteen. Again, the lower overall number of firms pursuing low cost strategies and those which are female-owned reflect earlier work in the small business field[22].

Specifically, for firms pursuing the low cost strategy, male business owners place greater emphasis on: the role of contributions in making pay decisions, keeping pay information secret, rewarding short term accomplishments, seniority's role in making pay decisions, and basing pay rates on a comparison of jobs within the firm. As discussed in earlier sections, these results are consistent with previous literature in the area. Dyer and Holder (1988), Fisher (1988), and Schuler and Jackson (1989) suggest that programming such as seniority recognition, focus on short term requirements and an internal focus on pay rate establishment are consistent with a low cost strategy. Further, male business owners tend to predominant in the low cost segment of small business[23]. The utilization of these programs by males in the low cost segment of this sample is consistent with this view.

Within the differentiation strategy firms, male business owners tend to emphasize job-based pay, seniority and the establishment of pay rates by comparing jobs within the firm. Female business owners tend to emphasize short term accomplishments and non-monetary rewards. No strong support for these findings is found in the literature, but, a closer examination of the findings across the strategies offer some results that merit further exploration.

Table 4.11: Compensation Programs by Gender Given Competitive Business Strategy

	Low Cost		
	Male (n=33)	Female (n=14)	t-Value
Contributions to firm impact pay	3.94	3.14	1.75*
Rates above competitors'	3.48	3.42	0.19
Rates below competitors'	2.55	2.50	0.13
Pay based on individual achievement	3.61	2.93	1.41
Job-based pay	3.93	3.25	1.46
Non-monetary rewards	2.41	3.36	-2.61**
Long term focus rewarded	3.44	3.42	0.07
Pay based on group achievements	2.90	2.67	0.62
Pay information secret in firm	4.06	3.15	1.92*
Short term focus rewarded	3.13	2.33	1.95*
Skill based pay	3.27	3.83	-1.18
Seniority impacts pay	3.34	2.57	1.99*
Pay rates compared to external market	3.06	2.83	0.50
Pay rates compared within firm	3.38	2.10	3.08**

*   Significant at the .10 level
**   Significant at the .05 level
*** Significant at the .01 level

Table 4.11 (continued)

| | Differentiation | | |
	Male (n=96)	Female (n=70)	t-Value
Contributions to firm impact pay	4.16	3.92	1.49
Rates above competitors'	3.60	3.49	0.58
Rates below competitors'	2.27	2.21	0.31
Pay based on individual achievement	3.87	3.99	-0.73
Job-based pay	3.27	2.73	2.67**
Non-monetary rewards	2.70	3.28	-3.14**
Long term focus rewarded	3.86	3.64	1.29
Pay based on group achievements	3.24	3.33	-0.49
Pay information secret in firm	4.29	4.15	0.83
Short term focus rewarded	2.80	3.23	-2.19**
Skill based pay	3.90	3.62	1.56
Seniority impacts pay	3.24	2.85	2.03**
Pay rates compared to external market	2.78	2.67	0.61
Pay rates compared within firm	3.02	2.55	2.27**

*   Significant at the .10 level
**   Significant at the .05 level
***   Significant at the .01 level

For example, whether the female business owner is pursuing a low cost or differentiation strategy, it seems she is given to utilizing non-monetary rewards in her compensation program far more often than a male business owner. Similarly, male business owners are more likely to emphasize seniority and individual contributions to a firm as well as to establish pay rates based upon an internal comparison of jobs irrespective of the strategy implemented. Such results suggest the need for further investigation as to whether some human resource programs when implemented in the small business area tend to be more gender driven than others and similarly, whether other programs tend to be more strategy driven.

Staffing

Table 4.12 presents the t-test results of staffing programs used by female and male business owners under differing competitive strategies. Support is especially limited in the low cost area. Here there are significant differences between men and women business owners' programming only in the males' use of a focus in hiring on a narrow skill range for candidates, and their utilization of personal referrals. Studies by Miles and Snow (1984), Dyer and Holder, (1988), Fisher (1988), and Schuler and Jackson (1989) suggest similar differences in programming.

Male business owners pursuing the differentiation strategy, in contrast, emphasize the use of agencies, both public and private, in their recruiting, utilize the interview and seek to match the potential of the individual to future organization needs in making a selection decision. Female business owners, on the other hand, emphasize the use of networks as recruiting sources, utilize personality tests, have formal written job descriptions on file and emphasize the "fit" between employee and firm in making hiring decisions.

Table 4.12: Staffing Programs by Owner Gender Given Competitive Business Strategy

| | Low Cost | | |
	Male	Female	t-Value
Ability tests	2.67	2.57	0.19
Biographical Information	4.45	4.07	0.91
Personality tests	1.52	1.64	-0.44
Interviews	4.91	4.43	1.23
Honesty tests	1.30	1.36	-0.25
Performance Tests	2.33	2.86	-0.94
References	4.33	3.50	1.67
Public agencies	2.27	1.62	0.64*
Private agencies	1.82	1.93	-0.31
Personal referrals	3.69	3.00	1.78*
Newspapers	3.42	3.21	0.42
Job fairs	1.12	1.14	-0.14
Electronic bulletin boards	1.00	1.00	———
Networking	2.58	2.21	0.76
Walk-ins	3.12	1.93	3.80***
Written job descriptions on file	2.48	3.44	-1.69
Job duties shaped by employees	3.21	3.08	0.32
Skills kept on file	2.38	2.38	-0.01
Firm forecasts numbers needed	2.84	3.15	-0.83
No guaranteed employment	3.73	3.55	0.34
Promotion from within policy	2.80	3.00	-0.52
Hire those with narrow skill range	2.27	1.62	1.80*
Informal testing used in selection	2.76	2.09	1.52
Hire based on match skills and job	4.33	4.57	-0.88
Hire based on fit	3.61	3.86	-0.92
Hire based on potential	3.73	3.92	-0.55

* Significant at the .10 level
** Significant at the .05 level
*** Significant at the .01 level

Table 4.12 (continued)

	Differentiation		
	Male	**Female**	**t-Value**
Ability tests	2.61	2.74	-0.55
Biographical Information	4.43	4.39	0.25
Personality tests	1.73	2.31	-2.70***
Interviews	4.96	4.79	1.83*
Honesty tests	1.56	1.64	-0.47
Performance Tests	2.79	2.84	-0.22
References	4.30	4.48	-1.37
Public agencies	2.49	2.06	2.28**
Private agencies	2.26	1.87	2.14**
Personal referrals	3.84	3.97	-0.89
Newspapers	3.25	3.29	-0.17
Job fairs	1.32	1.37	-0.45
Electronic bulletin boards	1.27	1.16	1.12
Networking	2.68	3.37	-3.04***
Walk-ins	3.03	3.19	-0.89
Written job descriptions on file	2.85	3.49	-2.72***
Job duties shaped by employees	3.20	3.25	-0.28
Skills kept on file	2.75	2.91	-0.83
Firm forecasts numbers needed	3.07	3.12	-0.23
No guaranteed employment	3.84	3.71	0.59
Promotion from within policy	3.06	2.97	0.43
Hire those with narrow skill range	2.08	2.13	-0.31
Informal testing used in selection	2.69	2.40	1.26
Hire based on match skills and job	4.17	4.11	0.36
Hire based on fit	3.73	4.06	-2.25**
Hire based on potential	3.95	3.57	2.50***

*   Significant at the .10 level
**   Significant at the .05 level
*** Significant at the .01 level

Given the literature in the area, there is support for the results. For example, much has been written regarding the interpersonal assets of women[24]. And indeed, networking, as a recruiting source, is utilized much more often by women than by men business owners.

Training and Development

Table 4.13 presents the t-test results examining training and development programming by owner's gender within a given competitive strategy. Specifically, within the low cost area, women business owners tend to utilize group dynamics training programs more than their male counterparts. Similarly, female owners tend to utilize training results to enhance current performance and assess the skills necessary for the future. Once more, the literature supporting this area is exceptionally limited.

Within the differentiation strategy, male business owners tend to gravitate toward programming based upon governmental regulations such as those created by the Occupational Safety and Health Act (OSHA). Women business owners are more likely to have a variety of uses for their training results including using them to train for current performance, for promotions and for future skill needs. Women also employ a greater variety of methods in their training (computer aided instruction, role playing, and on the job training) than their male counterparts. The work of Thompson and Hood (1991) reveals that women have a desire to help others, and these activities substantiate that nurturing role.

Table 4.13: Training and Development Programs by Owner Gender Given Competitive Business Strategy

	Low cost		
	Male (n=33)	**Female** (n=14)	**t-Value**
Training to improve performance	3.72	4.36	-1.98*
Training to teach future skills	2.87	3.71	-1.89*
Training to enhance promotability	3.16	3.46	-0.64
Training is government mandated	1.97	1.92	0.09
All employees eligible	4.09	4.54	-1.49
Training regularly scheduled	2.58	3.14	-1.35
Lectures	2.70	2.43	0.63
Videotapes	2.48	2.50	-0.05
Computer-aided instruction	1.82	2.00	-0.48
Role playing	1.48	1.79	-0.74
On the job training	4.55	4.29	0.76
Basic writing skills	2.06	2.46	-0.93
Oral communication skills	2.48	3.00	-1.12
Decision making skills	2.45	2.92	-0.93
Basic production skills	3.55	2.69	1.68
Quality skills	3.24	3.31	-0.13
Group dynamics skills	1.73	2.62	-1.88*
OSHA required training	2.97	2.67	0.62

*   Significant at the .10 level
**   Significant at the .05 level
***   Significant at the .01 level

Table 4.13 (continued)

| | Differentiation | | |
	Male (n=96)	Female (n=70)	t-Value
Training to improve performance	3.91	4.20	-1.76**
Training to teach future skills	3.28	3.77	-2.52***
Training to enhance promotability	3.10	3.52	-2.01**
Training is government mandated	2.15	1.80	1.69*
All employees eligible	3.95	3.93	0.10
Training regularly scheduled	2.86	3.38	-2.28**
Lectures	3.19	3.49	-1.29
Videotapes	2.83	3.15	-1.30
Computer-aided instruction	2.21	2.79	-2.81***
Role playing	2.09	2.97	-3.75***
On the job training	4.17	4.65	-3.00***
Basic writing skills	2.38	2.52	-0.66
Oral communication skills	2.78	3.26	-2.12***
Decision making skills	2.79	3.17	-1.87*
Basic production skills	3.24	2.91	1.55
Quality skills	3.42	3.26	0.74
Group dynamics skills	2.32	2.59	-1.33
OSHA required training	3.01	2.32	3.02***

* Significant at the .10 level
** Significant at the .05 level
*** Significant at the .01 level

Performance Appraisal

Table 4.14 presents the t-test results of performance evaluation programming by male and female business owners given the competitive strategy which they pursue. While they indicate some gender-based differences in programming, due to the limited treatment in the literature of performance appraisal by gender within small business, no statements can be made regarding their substantive contribution. However, in a more general sense, one can note that in all those instances where a performance appraisal programming element significantly differed between the sexes, regardless of the strategy employed, female business owners were far more likely to have emphasized it than their male counterparts. The fact that women business owners emphasized a greater variety of performance appraisal techniques (employees are evaluated on specific standards and evaluate themselves, use formal written techniques and carry out the exercise on a regular schedule) and had a greater variety of uses for the results of that appraisal (compensation and training and development) across all strategies suggests, to some degree, their focus on the development of the individual over a broader spectrum of abilities. This finding is consistent with the "nurturing" role in the literature that characterizes women[25].

Employee Relations

As the significance levels in Table 4.15 indicate, limited differences in employee relations programming by male and female business owners occur based upon the competitive business strategy chosen. In the low cost strategy area, female business owners tend to emphasize a worker-management committee more than their male counterparts. In the differentiation area, male business owners emphasize a multiple step grievance procedure with an outside arbitrator more than women do.

Table 4.14: Performance Appraisal Programs by Owner Gender Given Competitive Business Strategy

	Low Cost (n=47)		
	Male	**Female**	**t-Value**
Firm has formal written procedure	2.17	3.30	-1.84*
Results used for compensation	3.11	3.73	-1.71*
Results used for training	2.64	3.80	-3.21**
Results used for performance imp.	3.19	3.71	-1.42
Results used for staffing	2.93	3.25	-0.69
Evaluations regularly scheduled	2.80	4.00	-2.72**
Evaluation as a team	2.54	3.15	-1.62
Evaluation by specific standards	3.39	4.17	2.65**
Employees help determine standards	2.54	2.93	-0.96
Self evaluation	1.29	2.08	-2.29**
Supervisors evaluate	4.04	3.45	1.13
Customers evaluate	2.41	2.64	-0.54
	Differentiation (n=166)		
	Male	**Female**	**t-Value**
Firm has formal written procedure	3.23	3.55	-1.21
Results used for compensation	3.54	3.58	-0.21
Results used for training	3.12	3.66	-2.69**
Results used for performance imp.	3.86	3.88	-0.10
Results used for staffing	3.26	3.12	0.69
Evaluations regularly scheduled	3.26	3.97	-3.42**
Evaluation as a team	2.78	2.74	0.19
Evaluation by specific standards	3.44	3.76	-1.71*
Employees help determine standards	2.86	3.26	-1.79*
Self evaluation	2.39	3.24	-3.54**
Supervisors evaluate	3.99	4.14	-0.79
Customers evaluate	2.67	2.84	-0.66

*   Significant at the .10 level
**   Significant at the .05 level
*** Significant at the .01 level

Table 4.15: Employee Relations Programs by Owner Gender Given Competitive Business Strategy

	Low Cost		
	Male	**Female**	**t-Value**
Employee handbooks	2.70	2.50	0.42
Newsletters	1.58	1.43	0.53
Direct home mailings	1.39	1.43	-0.14
Internal memos	3.06	2.86	0.40
Meetings	3.94	4.07	-0.40
Bulletin board postings	3.09	2.50	1.36
Suggestion systems	2.55	2.71	-0.39
Open door policy	4.00	4.14	-0.42
Worker-management committee	2.18	3.07	-2.16**
Multiple step with outside arbitration	1.55	1.50	0.11
Multiple step with owner decision	3.06	3.85	-1.46
One step with owner decision	2.59	1.82	1.68
	Differentiation		
	Male	**Female**	**t-Value**
Employee handbooks	3.20	2.94	1.10
Newsletters	2.14	2.20	-0.31
Direct home mailings	1.53	1.38	1.23
Internal memos	3.50	3.44	0.29
Meetings	4.13	4.20	-0.54
Bulletin board postings	3.25	3.00	1.20
Suggestion systems	2.91	3.12	-1.05
Open door policy	4.32	4.29	0.20
Worker-management committee	2.68	2.76	-0.35
Multiple step with outside arbitration	1.65	1.31	2.21**
Multiple step with owner decision	3.16	3.39	-1.10
One step with owner decision	2.40	2.34	0.28

*   Significant at the .10 level
**   Significant at the .05 level
***   Significant at the .01 level

Overall Programmatic Assessment

Although the results on a function by function basis suggest, only slightly, a gender-based difference in programming, a distinctive pattern is emerging in the utilization of human resource programming across the functions given gender and competitive business strategy. Especially notable, are the differences between the levels of the items emphasized by each gender. Earlier, a number of differences, though statistically significant, were not meaningful given the magnitude of those differences.

The findings of this study's sample begin to provide empirical support for the descriptive/prescriptive work found in the literature[26]. In general, it appears that women business owners shape their human resource programming to emphasize the individual employee in a general sense while male business owners tend to concentrate on more firm-specific development. That is, women are more likely to emphasize, for example, training and development programs in their firms, while men are more likely to emphasize compensation like seniority systems and internal market pay setting.

The issue, raised earlier in this study, of whether female business owners are under represented in the low cost strategy area in this sample, was examined further through the use of crosstabulations. If gender impacts the choice of programming elements given a competitive business strategy, as the results of this study tend to suggest, the types of programming pursued by women within the low cost area may not be fully assessed. The crosstab results indicate little relationship between the business owner's gender and competitive business strategy chosen[27]. Thus, the results of this study do not help in clarifying this issue.

There is however, a relationship between the gender of business owners and whether they are in the manufacturing or service sectors of the economy[28]. Women comprised over 58% of the service sector (49 of 84 businesses) in this sample. This result is consistent with the findings of other studies[29]. Though not a focus of this study, the differences in programming by industry sector and industry sector and gender are viable areas for future investigation.

PROGRAMMING AND FINANCIAL PERFORMANCE

Compensation

Table 4.16 presents the t-test results of compensation programming in effective and ineffective financial performers given the competitive business strategy pursued by the firm. In the low cost area, effective financial performers tend to match or offer pay rates below those of their competitors, reward individual achievements, keep pay information secret and use skill based pay. These findings are consistent with those of earlier studies where low cost firms were found to emphasize tight cost control[30].

Within the differentiation area, pay secrecy and a short term focus were significant. Such a focus is in direct contrast to the long term perspective usually associated with this strategy[31]. However, as mentioned earlier, given the failure rate of small businesses, survival within a market niche may simply require the focus on a shorter time horizon regardless of the competitive strategy pursued.

Staffing

Within the staffing area, few significant differences were found based upon the effectiveness of the firm's financial performance. As Table 4.17 indicates, within the low cost area, successful firms were less likely to allow employees to shape their duties than their unsuccessful counterparts. However, they were more likely to utilize job fairs, networks and personal referrals as recruiting methods and personality tests as a selection device. The potential for some degree of cost control relative to, for example, a large scale external recruitment effort, may be offered as an explanation for this finding which is consistent with that posited in the literature[32].

Table 4.16: Compensation Programs by Performance Effectiveness Given Competitive Business Strategy

	Low Cost (n=47)		
	Effective	**Ineffec- tive**	**t- Value**
Contributions to firm impact pay	4.00	3.32	1.79*
Rates above competitors'	3.07	4.12	-3.09***
Rates below competitors'	2.85	2.00	3.09***
Pay based on individual achievement	3.85	2.74	2.75***
Job-based pay	3.71	3.81	-0.27
Non-monetary rewards	2.65	2.84	-0.57
Long term focus rewarded	3.61	3.20	1.14
Pay based on group achievements	3.04	2.53	1.55
Pay information secret in firm	4.26	3.21	2.73***
Short term focus rewarded	2.96	2.76	0.53
Skill based pay	3.70	2.94	1.85*
Seniority impacts pay	3.31	2.84	1.20
Pay rates compared to external market	2.96	3.12	-0.47
Pay rates compared within firm	3.27	2.67	1.42

*   Significant at the .10 level
**   Significant at the .05 level
***   Significant at the .01 level

Table 4.16 (continued)

	Differentiation (n=166)		
	Effective	Ineffec-tive	t-Value
Contributions to firm impact pay	4.01	4.19	-1.20
Rates above competitors'	3.64	3.39	1.23
Rates below competitors'	2.19	2.39	-0.91
Pay based on individual achievement	3.95	3.86	0.57
Job-based pay	3.08	2.98	0.48
Non-monetary rewards	2.94	2.98	-0.22
Long term focus rewarded	3.75	3.82	-0.42
Pay based on group achievements	3.36	3.08	1.45
Pay information secret in firm	4.33	4.02	1.65*
Short term focus rewarded	3.17	2.57	3.09***
Skill based pay	3.79	3.76	0.15
Seniority impacts pay	3.13	2.96	0.82
Pay rates compared to external market	2.83	2.52	1.54
Pay rates compared within firm	2.78	2.94	-0.75

*   Significant at the .10 level

**   Significant at the .05 level

***   Significant at the .01 level

Effective differentiation firms are more likely to emphasize ability tests as a selection device, use job fairs and networking as recruiting methods, and have policies that discourage hiring based upon a narrow skill range, but require written job descriptions.

Training and Development, Performance Appraisal and Employee Relations

Tables 4.18 through 4.20 present the results of training and development, performance appraisal and employee relations programming given the financial effectiveness of the firm within a given competitive strategy. An initial look at the training and development results within the low cost area appears problematic given that ineffective firms tend to emphasize training methods such as skill development in basic production and quality much more so than their effective counterparts. However, given that ineffective performers also emphasize offering training and development programming on a regular schedule, one could suggest that effective financial performers in the low cost area do not concentrate their efforts in training and development. To do so on a regular basis may not facilitate the tight cost control needed in this area. In short, these practices may contribute to the financial ineffectiveness.

In differentiation firms, where participation is emphasized, effective performers engage in a greater variety of training methods (lecture and role playing) covering participation enhancement skills (group dynamics and oral communication). Fostering participation is also seen in the performance appraisal programming conducted by these firms. Employees help determine appraisal standards, are evaluated regularly and engage in evaluation as an individual as well as a team member. In sum, there is only limited evidence of differences in human resource programming between effective and ineffective financial performers given the competitive business strategy pursued.

Table 4.17: Staffing Programs by Performance Effectiveness Given Competitive Business Strategy

	Low Cost (n=47)		
	Effective	**Ineffec-tive**	**t-Value**
Ability tests	2.93	2.21	1.62
Biographical Information	4.52	4.05	1.33
Personality tests	1.78	1.26	2.05**
Interviews	4.89	4.58	1.05
Honesty tests	1.37	1.26	0.67
Performance Tests	2.67	2.21	0.99
References	4.30	3.77	1.36
Public agencies	2.22	2.16	0.22
Private agencies	1.78	1.89	-0.36
Personal referrals	3.74	3.11	1.91*
Newspapers	3.59	3.16	1.03
Job fairs	1.15	1.00	2.13**
Electronic bulletin boards	1.00	1.00	——
Networking	2.81	1.84	2.63***
Walk-ins	2.96	2.58	1.30
Written job descriptions on file	2.70	2.77	-0.17
Job duties shaped by employees	2.93	3.59	-2.08**
Skills kept on file	2.43	2.32	0.31
Firm forecasts numbers needed	2.77	3.16	-1.17
No guaranteed employment	3.30	4.29	-2.59***
Informal testing used in selection	2.64	2.47	0.33
Hire based on fit	3.81	3.47	1.39
Hire those with narrow skill range	2.30	1.79	1.46
Hire based on matched skills and job	4.41	4.37	0.11
Hire based on potential	3.96	3.53	1.58
Promotion from within policy	2.71	3.05	-0.94

*   Significant at the .10 level
**   Significant at the .05 level
***   Significant at the .01 level

Table 4.17 (continued)

	Differentiation (n=166)		
	Effective	**Ineffec-tive**	**t-Value**
Ability tests	2.80	2.37	1.79*
Biographical Information	4.46	4.29	0.94
Personality tests	1.98	1.96	0.10
Interviews	4.91	4.82	0.86
Honesty tests	1.63	1.51	0.77
Performance Tests	2.87	2.69	0.74
References	4.37	4.40	-0.26
Public agencies	2.32	2.27	0.21
Private agencies	2.19	1.88	1.49
Personal referrals	3.86	3.98	-0.77
Newspapers	3.34	3.10	1.03
Job fairs	1.43	1.16	2.85***
Electronic bulletin boards	1.20	1.27	-0.50
Networking	3.13	2.61	1.96**
Walk-ins	3.10	3.10	-0.01
Written job descriptions on file	3.31	2.73	2.47**
Job duties shaped by employees	3.29	3.06	1.26
Skills kept on file	2.85	2.75	0.47
Firm forecasts numbers needed	3.17	2.89	1.08
No guaranteed employment	3.75	3.86	-0.46
Informal testing used in selection	2.61	2.46	0.66
Hire based on fit	3.93	3.73	1.29
Hire those with narrow skill range	1.97	2.40	-2.22
Hire based on matched skills and job	4.10	4.24	-0.92
Hire based on potential	3.80	3.76	0.24
Promotion from within policy	3.08	2.89	0.81

*   Significant at the .10 level
**   Significant at the .05 level
***   Significant at the .01 level

Table 4.18: Training and Development Programs by Performance Effectiveness Given Competitive Business Strategy

	Low Cost (n=47)		
	Effec-tive	Ineffec-tive	t-Value
Training to improve performance	3.77	4.11	-1.02
Training to teach future skills	2.88	3.53	-1.66*
Training to enhance promotability	2.88	3.79	-2.51**
Training is government mandated	1.67	2.26	-1.35
All employees eligible	4.23	4.26	-0.11
Training regularly scheduled	2.44	3.21	-2.20**
Lectures	2.59	2.74	-0.40
Videotapes	2.52	2.53	-0.02
Computer-aided instruction	1.78	2.05	-0.85
Role playing	1.81	1.26	2.07**
On the Job Training	4.48	4.63	-0.70
Basic writing skills	2.33	2.00	1.03
Oral communication skills	2.48	2.72	-0.70
Decision making skills	2.30	2.87	-1.57
Basic production skills	2.85	3.89	-2.22**
Quality skills	2.93	3.67	-1.83*
Group dynamics skills	2.11	1.83	0.80
OSHA required training	2.65	3.33	-1.63

*   Significant at the .10 level
**   Significant at the .05 level
***   Significant at the .01 level

Table 4.18 (continued)

| | Differentiation (n=166) | | |
	Effec-tive	Ineffec-tive	t-Value
Training to improve performance	4.08	3.89	1.07
Training to teach future skills	3.54	3.35	0.90
Training to enhance promotability	3.26	3.31	-0.25
Training is government mandated	1.90	2.23	-1.59
All employees eligible	4.00	3.80	0.97
Training regularly scheduled	3.26	2.63	2.59**
Lectures	3.44	3.02	1.80*
Videotapes	3.08	2.70	1.57
Computer-aided instruction	2.48	2.38	0.45
Role playing	2.62	2.08	2.51**
On the Job Training	4.37	4.38	-0.08
Basic writing skills	2.43	2.44	-0.02
Oral communication skills	3.10	2.70	1.75*
Decision making skills	2.98	2.88	0.48
Basic production skills	3.09	3.14	-0.24
Quality skills	3.39	3.26	0.54
Group dynamics skills	2.58	2.10	2.39**
OSHA required training	2.75	2.64	0.45

*   Significant at the .10 level
**   Significant at the .05 level
*** Significant at the .01 level

Table 4.19: Performance Appraisal Programs By Performance Effectiveness Given Competitive Business Strategy

	Low Cost		
	Effective	**Ineffec-tive**	**Ineffec-tive**
Firm has formal written procedure	2.24	2.82	-1.00
Results used for compensation	3.13	3.53	-1.08
Results used for training	2.90	2.92	-0.05
Results used for performance imp.	3.48	3.12	0.91
Results used for staffing	2.82	3.19	-0.86
Evaluations regularly scheduled	3.29	3.06	0.48
Evaluation as a team	2.67	2.82	-0.46
Evaluation by specific standards	3.67	3.53	0.45
Employees help determine standards	2.41	2.88	-1.30
Self evaluation	1.62	1.50	0.43
Supervisors evaluate	4.29	3.20	2.73***
Customers evaluate	2.61	2.27	0.87

*   Significant at the .10 level

**   Significant at the .05 level

***   Significant at the .01 level

Table 4.19 (continued)

	Differentiation		
	Effective	**Ineffec-tive**	**Ineffec-tive**
Firm has formal written procedure	3.54	3.00	1.92*
Results used for compensation	3.63	3.42	1.03
Results used for training	3.47	3.10	1.69*
Results used for performance imp.	3.85	3.89	-0.19
Results used for staffing	3.24	3.10	0.76
Evaluations regularly scheduled	3.74	3.15	2.57***
Evaluation as a team	2.87	2.52	1.70*
Evaluation by specific standards	3.60	3.51	0.50
Employees help determine standards	3.15	2.77	1.70*
Self evaluation	2.90	2.43	2.00**
Supervisors evaluate	4.15	3.83	1.62
Customers evaluate	3.47	3.10	1.27*

*   Significant at the .10 level
**   Significant at the .05 level
***   Significant at the .01 level

Table 4.20: Employee Relations Programs By Performance Effectiveness Given Competitive Business Strategy

	Low cost (n=47)		
	Effective	**Ineffec-tive**	**t-Value**
Employee handbooks	2.33	3.16	-1.90*
Newsletters	1.59	1.47	0.46
Direct home mailings	1.30	1.58	-1.13
Internal memos	3.07	2.95	0.32
Meetings	3.96	3.95	0.06
Bulletin board postings	2.73	3.05	-0.92
Suggestion systems	2.63	2.42	0.54
Open door policy	3.93	4.26	-1.15
Worker-management committee	2.52	2.32	0.55
Multiple step with outside arbitration	1.37	1.78	-1.08
Multiple step with owner decision	2.88	3.78	-2.01**
One step with owner decision	2.65	2.00	1.49

*   Significant at the .10 level
**   Significant at the .05 level
***   Significant at the .01 level

Table 4.20 (continued)

	Differentiation (n=166)		
	Effective	Ineffective	t-Value
Employee handbooks	3.23	2.80	1.64
Newsletters	2.26	1.94	1.48
Direct home mailings	1.47	1.45	0.17
Internal memos	3.54	3.33	1.03
Meetings	4.18	4.10	0.57
Bulletin board postings	3.18	3.06	0.56
Suggestion systems	2.82	3.38	-2.76***
Open door policy	4.32	4.29	0.13
Worker-management committee	2.75	2.63	0.47
Multiple step with outside arbitration	1.44	1.67	-1.09
Multiple step with owner decision	3.11	3.51	-1.51
One step with owner decision	2.35	2.45	-0.39

*   Significant at the .10 level
**   Significant at the .05 level
***   Significant at the .01 level

Previous studies have attempted to isolate the variables that impact performance in small business settings[33]. Accordingly, regression analysis is utilized here to examine the human resource programming elements which impact financial performance in the small business. The intent of the researcher was to discern which functional human resource area, if any, contributed the most to a firm's financial performance given its chosen competitive business strategy. That is, for example, are training and development programs key in differentiation firms in contrast to low cost firms where compensation programs predominate? Or is some other functional area paramount?

The objective measures of sales reported by participants were used as the dependent variable. Sales for the year prior to participation in the survey (1993) were reported   and have been   transformed logarithmically to overcome skewness. Fifty six percent (124 of 213) of those individuals responding to the questionnaire provided information on 1993 sales in their firms. Independent variables were chosen based upon their significance in previous t-tests[34].

Initially, a regression analysis was run across competitive business strategies to try to isolate human resource programming variables that impact overall financial performance. The results of this analysis are shown in Table 4.21.

Table 4.21: Regression Results Across Functions

Significant Variable	Effect	Significance
Handbook	+	.097
Customer Evaluates	+	.054
Training Lectures	+	.059
Job Fair	+	.067
Personality Tests	+	.021
Pay Secret	-	.027
Pay Above Competitors	-	.007

N= 124 cases

Total Variance Explained = 33%

As the results indicate, across the sample of small businesses, no specific human resource function has a predominate impact on financial performance. That is, variables in compensation, staffing, training and development, employee relations and performance appraisal have been isolated as impacting performance in this study.

A second set of regressions were run attempting to isolate those human resource programming variables that most impact financial performance given the chosen competitive business strategy. Table 4.22 presents results of the regression analysis for firms pursuing the differentiation strategy. Again, the intent of the researcher was to discern if a particular human resource function had the predominate impact on performance given the chosen strategy.

As the results suggest, no specific human resource function has a predominate effect on performance. Further, those programs which were isolated by this procedure as impacting performance come from each of the functional areas investigated in this study. The nature of the individual programs isolated differ from the overall assessment presented in Table 4.21. Specifically, the programs tend to focus on assessment and recognition of achievement from both an individual and group perspective. Further, the number of programs isolated as impacting performance in the differentiation area is greater than in the general case.

Table 4.22: Regression Results for Differentiation Firms

Significant Variable	Effect	Significance
Handbook	-	.062
Contributions' role in pay	+	.008
Employee self evaluation	+	.001
Team evaluation	+	.088
Formal written appraisal	+	.000
Individual achievements	+	.000
Owner multiple step	+	.049
Results for training	+	.000
Short term focus	+	.068
Pay secrecy	+	.000
Supervisor evaluations	+	.000
Training lectures	+	.045
Training via role play	+	.011

N = 99

Total Variance Explained = 47%

Finally, Table 4.23 presents results of regression analyses performed on low cost firms. These findings reiterate earlier discussion on the relationship between human resource programming and competitive business strategy. As noted in the initial training and development section of this chapter, low cost firms focus little attention on training and development issues beyond those which are government mandated. Indeed, no training and development programs have been isolated from this sample which impact the financial performance of these low cost firms.

Table 4.23: Regression Results for Low Cost Firms

Significant Variable	Effect	Significance
Contributions role in pay	-	.099
Self evaluation	+	.033
Owner multiple step	-	.005
Personality test	+	.041
Supervisor evaluation	-	.042

N=25

Total Variance Explained = 12%

NOTES

1. General information on human resource programming is provided by Fombrum, Tichy and Devanna (1984), Schuler (1992), Schuler and MacMillan (1984) and Schuler and Jackson (1989). Balkin and Gomez-Mejia (1987) focus on compensation elements. Olian and Rynes (1984) look at staffing programs. Training and development is examined by Deshpande and Golhar (1994). McEvoy (1984) and Holoviak and DeCenzo (1982) look at performance appraisal.

2. Though Balkin and Gomez-Mejia utilized a growth-maintenance paradigm for measuring competitive business strategy, Segrev (1989) has found empirical convergence between the work of Miles and Snow (1978) and Porter (1980). Thus the results for the Balkin/Gomez-Mejia growth group would be similar to the findings for a differentiation group.

3. Milkovich and Boudreau also note that skill-based pay predominates in small business. Since small business predominately pursues a differentiation strategy, it follows that skill-based is common in a differentiation setting.

4. Dyer and Holder 9188), Fisher (1989) and Schuler and Jackson (1989) present examples appropriate for differentiation.

5. The Miles and Snow typology (1978) consists of Prospectors, Defenders and Analyzers.

6. Gupta (1986) is one such researcher.

7. Empirical work in the managerial selection area has been completed by Gerstein and Reisman (1983), Kerr (1982), Leontiades (1982), Wissema, Van Der Pol and Messer (1980) and Szilagyi and Schweiger (1984).

8. See Schuler and Jackson (1989).

9. McEvoy (184) is one notable exception.

10. Brush (1995), p. 29.

11. As per the findings of Schuler and Jackson (1989).

12. Hisrich and O'Brien (1982).

13. See Cooper, Gimeno-Gascon and Woo (1994), Roure and Keeley (1990), Chaganti and Schneer (1994), Hisrich and Brush (1983), and Box, Watts and Hisrich (1994).

14. See a study by The National Foundation for Women Business Owners (1994) for other obstacles to business start-up for women business owners.

15. This finding is rather consistent in research in this area. See Hisrich and Brush (1985), Chaganti (1986), Honig-Haftel and Martin (1986) and Brush (1995).

16. See Kohlberg (1981) and Gilligan (1982) for extensive discussions of the socialization of girls and women.

17. The woman's role of nurturer is found in the research of Salganicoff (1990), Powell (1988), Lipman (1984), Chorodow (1978) and Miller (1976).

18. See Gillis-Donovan and Moynihan-Bradt (1990).

19. Cooper, Gimeno-Gascon and Woo (1994), Roure and Keely (1990) and Box, Watts and Hisrich (1994).

20. Salganicoff (1990) and Powell (1988).

21. Salganicoff (1990), Powell (1988), Lipman (1984), Chorodow (1978) and Miller (1976).

22. Williams, Carter and Reynolds (1993).

23. Williams, Carter and Reynolds (1993).

24. Hisrich and Brush (1985), Smith, McCain and Warren (1982) and Brush (1995).

25. Salganicoff (1990), Powell (1988), Lipman (1984), Chorodow (1978) and Miller (1976).

26. Miles and Snow (1984) and Brush (1995).

27. Crosstabulation of gender by competitive business strategy yielded the result: Chhi square equal 2.35, $p < .13$.

28. Crosstabulation of gender by industry orientation (service/manufacturing): Chi-square equal 7.64, $p< .005$.

29. *The State of Small Business, 1994.*

30. Dyer and Holder (1988).

31. Schuler and Jackson (1989).

32. Dyer and Holder (1988) and Schuler and Jackson (1989).

33. See Cragg and King (1988) and Begley and Boyd (1986).

34. Cragg and King (1988).

CHAPTER 5

Toward a New Model of Human Resource Strategy

A REVIEW OF THE FINDINGS

The purpose of this study was to examine the concept of a human resource strategy and to ascertain what types of human resource strategies could be found in small businesses. Human resource strategy development, as a means to building a competitive advantage for the firm, is a recent focus of efforts in the human resource field. However, those efforts have been hampered by a lack of an operational definition for the concept and empirical work supporting it.

This study combined Hofer and Schendel's strategic hierarchy (1978) from the strategic management literature with the descriptive work on human resource strategy in the human resource field to develop a multi-level concept. Thus human resource strategy was measured at two levels (business and functional levels) for purposes of this research. Business human resource strategy was the intended goals for human resources that help the organization achieve a competitive advantage. Functional human resource strategy was the means by which the organization implemented the business human resource strategy.

Business human resource strategy was assessed by human resource priorities. Such priorities are the primary human resource orientations or concerns of the firm. It is to these concerns that the firm attaches the most importance and these which direct its decision-making with regard to its employees. Functional human resource strategy, on the other hand, was measured by specific programs, plans and practices utilized in the human resource area. These programs are the means by which the business human resource strategy is implemented.

Early descriptive work in the human resource field suggests that competitive business strategy is a major determinant of human resource strategy. Thus, the types of human resource priorities emphasized by a firm should differ based upon its choice of competitive business strategy. The results of this study show an overall relationship between human resource priorities and competitive business strategy, however no clear pattern in specific human resource priorities is discernible even though a limited number of priorities do differ depending on the competitive business strategy of the company. Firms pursuing differentiation emphasized a creative, innovative approach to job tasks, commitment to the company and a focus on the outcome of a process. Their low cost counterparts, in contrast, emphasized a constant, predictable approach to job tasks, commitment to the job itself and a focus on the rules and procedures of a process. Although no discernible pattern in the priorities as per a competitive business strategy was detected by the researcher, discriminant analysis did correctly identify the competitive business strategy utilized by a firm given its human resource priority dimensions, in 73 percent of the cases.

The small business arena has recently begun to focus on the differences between male and female business owners in the development and management of their firms. Accordingly, human resource priorities were assessed for gender effects. Although individual priorities differ by gender, no clear pattern of priorities emerged given the gender of the firm owner. Specifically, male business owners emphasize an employee's limited personal accountability for job duties and a constant, predictable approach to those duties. Women business owners, on the other hand, emphasize greater personal accountability by employees for their job duties and a creative, innovative approach to tasks.

When gender differences in human resource priorities were investigated within specific competitive business strategies, again no clear pattern of priorities emerged. In the low cost firms, males emphasized job flexibility and the outcomes of the job. In the differentiation area, women business owners emphasized job flexibility, independent behavior, personal accountability and creative job approaches.

Given the findings of this study, human resource priorities do seem to differ based upon the choice of competitive business strategy made by the small business owner. However, the ability to delineate a specific profile of priorities per competitive business strategy is limited given small businesses' differing interpretation of priorities. Such a result questions whether human resource priorities exist in a small business and/or whether competitive business strategy is a determinant of priority choice in the small firm.

With regard to the former question, a retrospective look at the case study interviews that comprised the first part of this research project[1], provide insights as to the interpretation of the questionnaire results. Here those interviews suggest that small business owners do have priorities, albeit ones that are not clearly articulated in their minds.

> "I really want all these things from my employees, but it depends on the day, the task at hand, the individual and a [bunch] of other factors which really come into play at a time. If I really sit and think about it, I can answer you that I absolutely want this one or that one all the time for the whole business. I guess I just don't think about it."

Such a statement suggests that an underlying orientation for managing human resources is present, even in a small business. However, that emphasis is not often clearly articulated by the owner given the need to manage his firm. In short, the small business owner is not able (due to time constraints or simply a lack of interest) to step back and view his decision making with regard to his human resources in a larger, more general sense.

Such a "failure" to view decisions from a more general perspective with regard to human resource priorities also leads one to question whether small business owners are able to articulate clearly their firm's competitive business strategy. This study chose to focus on competitive business strategy as the chief determinant of human resource strategy given empirical work in the discipline. However, the results of the descriptive field work done in phase one of this project, suggest that other factors, including owner values and stage of the firm's life cycle, might impact the pattern of human resource priorities found. Assessment of such factors is not possible given the design of this study, but could be considered in future work in this area.

Functional human resource strategy was also examined in light of the competitive business strategy chosen by the firm's owner. When human resource functions are examined individually for programming differences by competitive business strategy chosen, few significant differences emerge. If, however, these same programming elements are viewed across human resource functions, using an analysis technique devised by the researcher[2], a rudimentary pattern emerges. Firms pursuing a differentiation strategy tend to utilize human resource programming that focuses largely on procedural issues. That is, such firms emphasize specific practices within the staffing area with regard to their recruiting sources (walk-ins, personal referrals), and selection devices (personality and honesty tests and job fairs); the training and development area with regard to training methods (computer-aided, lecture, videotapes, role playing); and in the employee relations area with regard to the type of communication methods utilized (handbooks, memos, newsletters and suggestion systems). Unfortunately, a comparison between the pattern of programming within differentiation and low cost firms can not be made, given this sample's lack of significant programming elements within the low cost area.

The inability to assess a clear pattern in the human resource programming in a low cost strategy firm merits further discussion. Given the fairly substantial number of programming differences across human resource functions found within the differentiation firms, one could conclude that differences in programming do exist between the two groups of firms. Further, one could argue that the programmatic elements utilized in this study, though substantiated by pre-testing[3], are simply not appropriate to the activities of small businesses pursuing low cost strategies and thus prevent the researcher from clearly delineating those specific differences. Indeed, a body of small business literature argues that the low cost strategy (from a Porter perspective) is not a viable competitive option for small firms due to the inability to create and benefit from economies of scale. Accordingly, the definition of competitive business strategy chosen for this study may be inappropriate and a different typology may need to be utilized in future analysis to better assess subtle programming differences between the strategic types.

The pattern of human resource programming utilized by women business owners does differ from that used by male business owners. Again, a limited number of significant differences are found on a function by function basis. However, when the differences are aggregated across the human resource function a distinctive gender-based pattern begins to emerge.

In general, women business owners adopt a pattern of human resource programming that suggests the individual employee is a resource to the firm. Such a pattern is especially noticeable when gender-based programming differences are examined within specific competitive strategies. Female business owners are much more likely to emphasize a wider variety of human resource programs than are male business owners. Given the number of significant differences in specific functional areas, it appears that men concentrate few efforts in the training and development, employee relations and performance appraisal areas.

Those programs emphasized by women business owners have both policy and procedural elements. Male business owners generally emphasize programs which are procedural in nature. The resulting profile suggests that women program to develop the individual in a general, "human capital"[4] sense. That is, women-owned firms are more likely to have programs in training and development, for example, that develop generally transferable skills such as decision making and group dynamics. Male business owners, in contrast, program for a more "firm-specific" effect, being more likely to offer basic production skills and OSHA-mandated training.

No clear pattern emerged with regard to programming among effective and ineffective financial performers given the competitive business strategy they pursued. While significant differences are found on a human resource function by function basis, no distinct overall pattern is evident.

The question of alignment was also difficult to address due to the lack of a distinct priority or programming pattern in effective and ineffective financial performers. Nonetheless, when specific human resource priorities that were significant are examined in light of specific human resource programming elements that were also significant, one can discern some degree of "fit" between the two. For example, in the low cost strategy, commitment to the job was considered a priority. To facilitate performance in that job, basic production skills training was emphasized. While this assessment is made from a rather subjective perspective, it does suggest the need to more closely examine this issue in future studies.

Analysis of variance results suggest that competitive business strategy and gender are not related to performance in the sample's small businesses. However, regression analyses indicate that human resource programming does account for some of the variance in performance. These findings suggest that further attention must be given to the types of human resource programming being carried out in small businesses. At the same time, a re-assessment of the way strategy is viewed in the small business must be undertaken.

In sum, the research questions raised earlier can now be addressed:

What types of human resources strategies are found in small businesses?

Whether human resource strategy exists at the business level in the small firm is unclear. Some significant differences in priorities are found when the competitive business strategy differs, but a distinct pattern is not apparent.

There do seem to be human resource strategies at the functional level in the firm. In firms pursuing the differentiation competitive strategy, there is a focus on procedure in each of the human resource functional areas although the outcome or orientation of that procedure is unclear based on the data in this study. The pattern for low cost firms is not clear. Further work in this area is thus recommended.

Does gender influence the type of human resource strategy chosen by a small business?

It would appear that the gender of the business owner impacts the type of functional human resource strategy in the firm. Women tend to develop functional human resource strategies that focus on both policy and procedure with an orientation toward the development of the employee as "human capital". Male business owners seem to develop their functional human resource strategies for "firm-specific" usage.

Is the choice of human resource strategy related to a small business' performance?

It does appear that functional human resource strategy impacts firm performance although its specific impact is unclear. Regression results indicate that between 8% and 47% of the variance in performance can be accounted for by human resource programming elements given the particular competitive business strategy chosen.

RESEARCH QUESTION: ALIGNMENT

Earlier, a supplementary research question was posed:

"Given a firm classified as an effective performer, what is the relationship between the human resource priorities used by that firm and the human resource programs utilized?"

It is difficult to speak to the question of alignment given the lack of a general profile of human resource priorities and programs. However, Deshpande and Golhar (1994), suggest that such a finding is not uncommon. Large and small manufacturing firms were found to lack personnel policies that reinforced the workforce characteristics important for the success of the firm. Specifically, Deshpande and Golhar (1994) found that workers needed to be able to inspect their work within the organizations studied, yet no incentive systems supporting that action were established by the firm. Gatewood and Feild (1987) also note the difficulty small businesses have in maintaining "behavioral consistency" (p.17) in such programming as personnel selection.

When effective versus ineffective firms were examined across competitive business strategies for differences in their human resource priorities, no significant results were found. However, given a competitive business strategy, specific priorities did emerge as significant, and can be examined in relationship to specific human resource programming also found to be significant within that competitive strategy.

For example, in the low cost area, individual behavior is emphasized as is commitment to the job. An analysis of human resource programming found to be significant within the low cost area reveals that effective firms tend to reward individual achievement. The focus on the individual suggests an attempt to "fit" programs to the priorities emphasized.

In the differentiation area, effective performers emphasize commitment to the organization. Again, no other priorities were found to be significant, eliminating the possibility of a profile. Once more, analysis of significant programming elements provide some indication of alignment between the two areas. In the performance appraisal area, employees are given the opportunity to help determine the standards on which they will be evaluated and even are permitted to perform some self-evaluation. These two activities allow the employee to feel a sense of ownership in the program itself. That sense of ownership is readily translated into a feeling of commitment to the firm to which they belong. The issue of alignment can not, however, be clearly addressed given the findings of this study.

This research project was exploratory in nature, but does provide some basis for a continuing examination of the issue of human resource strategy. Further, it provides some new data for consideration in the small business field and suggests that women business owners are a viable focus of future research.

LIMITATIONS OF THE STUDY

As in any study, this research effort is subject to certain general and specific limitations which restrict the applicability and ability to generalize its findings. The following are several of the key limitations of this study.

Representativeness of Sample

The firms participating in this study were drawn from client lists of Small Business Development Centers (SBDCs) located throughout the country, members of The National Education Center for Women in Business, Pennsylvania TEC/Small Business United, and the Pittsburgh chapter of the National Association of Women Business Owners. Respondents are fairly evenly distributed throughout the country with the Northwest and Southwest being those regions most underrepresented.

Thus, the overall sample is not representative of the population of small businesses in general in so far as the client lists of participating organizations are not representative of that population. Such a possibility exists in that businesses desiring membership in all but the SBDCs must pay a membership fee. Further, anecdotal evidence suggests that those firms seeking assistance from the SBDC network have a higher failure rate than small businesses in general[5].

Research Design

This study relied heavily upon the responses to a questionnaire. This questionnaire was to be completed only by the owner of a small business. If, perchance, an employee of the firm completed the survey instead of the owner, perceptual differences could be introduced that might impact subsequent data analysis.

Accuracy of the Data

Related to the issue of research design is the nature of the data collected. This survey required there be only one respondent per organization. The data requested from that individual was self-report, almost exclusively perceptual data. As such, the actual states of the variables as measured may differ from the manner in which they are perceived. In short, one can not discern how accurately the reported data reflects actual organization conditions.

Sample Size

Although the overall sample size of this study is acceptable, the number of female business owners pursuing a low cost strategy is clearly problematic. The small sample size may be due to the manner in which competitive business strategy is measured or it may be a result of an actual aversion on the part of women business owners to pursuing that strategy. In sum, questions arise as to the overall representativeness of the female, low cost firms in this sample.

Measure Limitations

The results of this study are also subjected to the limitations of specific measures utilized in the questionnaire.

Competitive Business Strategy. This study employed a single self-report measure of competitive business strategy. Although the self-report measure correlates with a scale of competitive business strategy (based on work of Davis and Dess, 1984), Venkatraman and Grant (1984) argue that single item scales are appropriate only for single trait variables. As noted earlier in this document, strategy is viewed as multi-dimensional (Hambrick, 1980) by most researchers in the field with the notable exception of Gupta and Govindarajan (1984).

Human Resource Priorities. A four point scale was utilized in the human resource priority section to facilitate respondents in assessing their placement on each dimension of the human resource priorities. The use of a Likert five point scale would have effected greater differentiation in the responses given.

A second aspect of the priority scales has to do with the uni-dimensionality of each trait listed. Some scales may be questionable as to whether they present a continuum of a single trait or multiple traits.

In so far as some study participants may view the dimensions presented as multi-trait in nature, the responses may over-report some dimensions at the expense of others.

Human Resource Programming. Human resource programming was developed in light of research carried out in mostly corporate settings. In that specific human resource functions are not transferable from the corporate to small business setting, or specific programming elements are inappropriate, the findings will underrepresent certain dimensions and overrepresent others.

Organization Performance. While the performance measures utilized here circumvent certain measurement problems, as noted earlier, they are subject to other limitations. First, each respondent was asked to indicate, on a five-point, Likert-type scale, the degree to which he/she is satisfied with the performance of the small business based upon a group of performance criteria. Reporting performance in such a manner, however, allows for underperforming firms to appear to be performing better than they are, with overperforming firms appearing to be performing worse than they are. In short, differences between desired and actual performance are not fully addressed given the use of this technique.

MODEL REVISION

The findings of this study as well as the limitations in measures and methods noted in the previous section suggest the need to re-examine and revise the original model proposed for this project. The original model was developed based upon an extensive review of the literature; a literature that was largely based at the corporate level. Initial field testing both through interviews and questionnaires indicated the legitimacy of such a model. However, given the results of this study, it would appear that the corporate model, while a viable starting point for analysis, is an inadequate model for examining the small business area. Specifically, differences in aspects of the human resource strategy appear to, at times, be based on characteristics of the owner, and not, competitive strategy-based.

The original model of human resource strategy (Figure 5.2) suggests that competitive strategy determines the business human resource strategy which then drives the choice of programming at the functional level. The revised model (Figure 5.3) emphasizes the impact of owner characteristics on all aspects of human resource strategy in the small business area. Specifically, in the small business arena, the business owner's personal characteristics (including, but not limited to, gender and past business experience) impacts the choice of business[6], the competitive strategy pursued within that area, and the subsequent human resource programming.

This study concentrated on the owner characteristic of gender. Study results indicate the first area in which gender has an impact is in the choice of business. Summary reviews of small business widely cite the differences in industry concentration between male and female owners[7]. Males tend to be found in the manufacturing sector of the economy and women heavily center in the service sector. Small Business Administration statistics indicate that women own 40% of all proprietorships in the wholesale and retail trade category and 39% of all those in the service sector[8]. Whether this concentration is due to gender (and gender based discrimination or societal pressures), experience (males have traditionally been employed in the manufacturing sector), or some other factor, owner characteristics do suggest differing choices as to the line of business pursued.

Table 5.1: Industry Concentration by Gender

	Service	Manufacturing	
Male	49 (38%)	80 (62%)	129 (60.6%)
Female	49 (58%)	35 (42%)	84 (39.4%)
Totals	98 (46%)	115 (54%)	213

As Table 5.1 indicates, this study's breakdown of business types by gender also indicates that women are more apt to be owners of service-oriented firms.

The revised model also suggests that the choice of business impacts the chosen competitive business strategy. A retrospective review of the anecdotal information from the interviews of phase one, however, suggest that the paradigm of competitive strategy developed by Porter and utilized at the outset of this study is too limiting for the small business arena, particularly with regard to the service sector of small business. Interview data that previously seemed to describe only isolated circumstances assumes new, clearer meaning when coupled with the results of the questionnaire phase. As such, the interview data suggests a much richer, more detailed typology of competitive business strategy based upon the focus and differentiation dimensions of Porter may be more appropriate for the small business arena. Information from the owners of two Italian restaurants, interviewed in phase one, provide insight on this issue:

"By the very nature of our business, we are niche players—so it's a given we're focus strategy guys. But, you have to look further or you don't know anything about the company."

The two restaurants are located directly across the street from one another. Both cater to family diners, delivering quality food at moderate prices. So what differentiates one from the other?

"Quality is such a misused term now. We've had quality food for 35 years now. You wouldn't still be in the restaurant business if you didn't. So why does one person come here, and the other there? I think we provide a friendlier atmosphere than [ ] across the way. You know, we don' t just bring food, we also bring a service to your table. Six of my twelve waitresses worked for my dad here 20 years ago. They're like family. They also treat our customers the same way. You know, they bring you your spaghetti and then stand and chat. [ ] is such a "mother hen" to everyone that you'll order the sampler platter and she'll say, 'That's too expensive, order something else." Across the street they bring your dinner and anything else you want, then step back and let you eat—but constantly watch to fill your water glass or coffee cup. How do we compete? Us—friendly service. Them—"professional", ("la-de-da") but "removed" service. (Note: quotes in final sentence reflect emphasis placed by speaker.)

That Porter's generic competitive business strategy typology[9] may not fully capture the richness of small business' strategies is further illustrated in the case of two family-owned, non-franchise grocers located in adjacent shopping plazas. Upon questioning, each owner described his strategy to be one of low cost. Both heavily emphasize low prices through weekly specials and the use of double coupons.

Further discussion, however, indicated that some refinement of the term "low cost" may be needed.

"I really get low cost across to my customer as my strategy. I just recently revised my BOGO (Buy one, get one free) policy to make my prices even lower. BOGOs are now available here on each item in the set. That means if I'm chargin' two for $4.40, I really charge $2.20 each. I re-programmed my computer to do that to benefit my customers. Before, the thing was programmed to charge $4.40 for the first one and $.00 for the second. Then you only benefited if you bought two. Now you get savings even if you buy only one. This split pricing really benefits the customer and proves my low cost strategy to them. The guy next door relies solely on bulk buying for his low prices. That makes us lower.

A further retrospective analysis of interview data suggests that the variety of competitive business strategy types may be greater in service oriented firms than in their manufacturing counterparts, particularly with regard to those firms pursuing the low cost strategy. A crane company owner discussed his competitive business strategy:

"We are recognized as an overall low cost leader. Everyone knows we don't build as large a profit margin into our bids for job specs [specifications], and yet, we can still deliver the highest quality product around."

A machine shop owner echoed his thoughts:

We compete on low cost. There are a number of people who have places like mine, all making stuff like us, all within a short drive. Yet, everyone comes to me 'cause I can get it to you at a low price. I run a lean and mean shop to keep it that way and we've been real good at it."

In summary, it appears that, especially with regard to service oriented small businesses, the typology of competitive business strategy based upon Porter's work (1980) is limited. A richer, more detailed typology is needed to capture the nuances of the small firm. A review of the interview material from phase one of this study suggests a variety of possible options. Small businesses seem to focus their energies on differentiating themselves from their competitors on the basis of: location, uniqueness of product, type of product, atmosphere, amount of customer service, type of customer service, quality of service, quality of product, age of business ("They come here because we've been here forever—we're dependable."), and low cost. If the competitive business strategy typology is refined along these lines, with low cost being one possible option of the differentiation strategy, the measure might capture more of the distinction between small firms and how they operate.

The preceding list of possible small business competitive strategies is limited due to the small number of interviews conducted in phase one. That aside, "re-analyzing" the interviews do provide a basis for further investigation. Accordingly, development of this idea will require assessment of firm activities on a much larger scale under more methodologically rigorous conditions than those employed here.

The revised model also suggests that gender has some impact on the choice of competitive business strategy pursued by the business owner. An exceptionally low percentage of female business owners indicate that they pursue a low cost strategy in their businesses. Such a low percentage of the total sample may indicate problems with the manner in which competitive business strategy is being measured. To address this potential problem of external validation of a self report measure, a scale of strategy dimensions derived from the work of Davis and Dess (1984) was included in this study. The correlations between the two measures of competitive business strategy was .69. Thus the problem is not in the way in which the strategy is being assessed, but in the measure itself. A delineation in strategy between low cost and differentiation is not appropriate for the small business arena given this study's sample. That is, it appears from the results of this study, that women rarely choose low cost as the basis of their competitive strategy.

The revised model also incorporates information from the small business literature (reviewed again after the questionnaire findings), suggesting that previous experience impacts the choice of business by an individual[10]. Further, this experience may impact the type of strategy pursued by the firm[11] and the success of the firm[12], as well as specific programming carried out in the firm[13]. Case study information from the initial phase of this study lends support for these findings. A woman business owner indicated that one way in which she differentiates her firm from her competitors is that hers is a certified woman-owned business[14], a designation which especially assists firms in government procurement. In contrast, the owner of a firm specializing in industrial crane construction suggested that he brought to his firm, "what I have learned is right and wrong in this area over the past thirteen years".

Though this owner characteristic was not assessed directly in the questionnaire phase of this study due to space limitations, future analysis should further address this issue. That is, more work needs to be done to ascertain whether certain competitive business strategies are not used by women business owners because they choose businesses for which those strategies are inappropriate, or if those competitive business strategies are avoided because women are not able to manage on that basis.

As with the original model, the revised model suggests that competitive business strategies are the basis of the priorities set by business owners for their employees. Once more analysis of interview data coupled with this study's empirical data suggest that the priorities utilized in this study need to be adjusted for usage in the small business arena.

As noted in Chapter 3 of this document, a chi-square test indicated that human resource priorities are different for each competitive strategy. However, when t-tests were run on each individual priority to assess how it differed based upon the chosen competitive business strategy, few significant differences were found. A closer look at the t-test results in conjunction with interview information indicates the small business perspective on priorities differs from its corporate counterpart which was the basis of this model.

It is instructive to examine the magnitude of emphasis indicated by the small business owner for each priority in the questionnaire (See Table 3.1). Although some of the differences are statistically significant between the emphasis in priority, given the competitive business strategy, generally the distinction is minimal. For example, almost no numerical difference exists between the mean for personal accountability between low cost and differentiation competitors (3.45 versus 3.50). As discussed earlier, such findings raise the question as to whether human resource priorities are a meaningful concept in the small business area. The answer, unequivocally, is "yes". Each small business owner interviewed could, after some thought, clearly articulate what he "needed to get from his employees in order to compete". This suggests that small business owners, do have priorities, they simply have not articulated them to the extent their corporate counterparts have.

Information from the interviews further suggests that the definition of the priority in a small business setting is sometimes, substantially different that that held in the corporate setting. The issue of efficiency being related to economies of scale in the corporate setting versus the ability to move between jobs in the small firm, is just one example. The owner of the grocery store mentioned earlier where items were re-priced in the computer system to benefit customers defined "commitment" in a small business setting:

> "I need commitment from my workers to come to their jobs in this company everyday, so I am midway on this scale. I need people in "place", like at the cash register. Do they have to be committed to their job? I don't know. To be honest, a monkey could scan the products. But, I need them to come to work everyday and put on a smiling face for the firm so that those shoppers come back next week. You can't believe the people that won't even do that much. Like the high school bag boys or stockers whose moms are always calling them off. That's not commitment to either job or company. So, if they would pick either one as their focus, it would sure help me."

The nature of small business human resource priorities needs to be assessed further. As with the competitive strategy chosen, finer distinctions in each priority definition need to be made and clearly conveyed to future study participants. For example, efficiency is a consistent focus in the small business setting given the generally limited opportunity for waste of any sort. Yet the concept of efficiency could vary in the small business setting between getting a long line of customers through a check-out quickly (efficient usage of time) to meeting those same customers' needs in various store departments (a deli counter worker who can get customers their bake goods from the bakery and then get them their luncheon meats (efficiency in the use of human resources).

Though this general distinction in priority perspectives has been discernible in the interview data, specific examples of priorities and their explicit definition are very limited. A much more detailed study is necessary to fully develop the issue of priorities in the small business setting.

Analysis of variance results suggest that competitive business strategy is not related to performance. In light of this finding, interview data from the initial phase of this study has new meaning. This data suggests that a different typology for describing the strategies utilized by small businesses may be developed by focusing on the specific ways in which firms differentiate themselves in the marketplace. Firm owners discussed "quality", "location", "uniqueness of product", and "atmosphere/experience" as ways in which they differentiated themselves from their competitors. Consequently, differences in priorities and programming among the strategy types may be more pronounced., and a clearer relationship between competitive business strategy and performance found.

Although analysis suggests that strategy should not be considered a chief determinant, this model maintains its importance although there is a need to re-assess the manner in which it is measured. Further, though some analysis suggests that gender is not related to performance, the differences found in programming based upon the gender of the business owner weigh heavily in its inclusion here.

In sum, the revised model suggests that specific owner characteristics, including gender and past experience are the chief determinants of the competitive strategy within the small business. The choice of that strategy then drives the choices made with regard to human resource priorities and programs. The relationship between those priorities and programs impacts the firm's performance.

IMPLICATIONS/DIRECTIONS FOR FUTURE RESEARCH

The findings of this research have implications for the human resource, small business and public policy areas.

Human Resource Management

It has been posited, most notably by Dyer (1984), that human resource strategy is a multi-level concept. Given the results of this study, assessment of any levels beyond the functional should be carried out in corporate settings.

The concepts of human resource priorities utilized in this study, while understood by small business owners, simply did not capture the orientations they had toward their employees. As noted in the limitations section, the measure of human resource priorities used in this study could be inappropriate given the time pressures small business owners face. That is, while owners are very capable of discussing the types of human resource programming they utilize in their firms, they have not taken the time to discern the basic orientation underlying each program or policy. As such, it may be beneficial in future studies of human resource strategy at the small business level, to obtain data regarding programming and from that data, determine the underlying priorities.

An alternative means of addressing the human resource priorities of the business owner might be to assess his/her values. The concept of values is more clearly articulated in the literature and better understood by the general populace than that of human resource priorities. The underlying orientation of human resource priorities as assessed through interviews in this study is very close to the concepts reviewed by Guth and Taguiri (1965)[15].

The difficulties encountered in assessing human resource priorities also suggests that much work still needs to be done in the field to create an operational definition of human resource strategy. The multi-dimensional nature of the concept needs to be more clearly articulated.

Given the regression results of this study, human resources does seem to play a role in the performance of the small business. What that role is in the small business needs to be re-assessed especially with regard to individual human resource functions. Further, comparisons between the impact human resource strategy has on performance in the small firm and its impact in the large firm must be made. If findings similar to those in this study occur, the potential for human resource management to provide a competitive advantage to the small firm can be developed.

Small Business

The overwhelming significance of this research endeavor lies in its contributions to the small business area. Many practitioners suggest that small businesses operate without clearly defined programs and that those programs in place bear little relationship to one another. The results of this study clearly indicate however, that small businesses do have recognizable human resource practices that mold into compensation, staffing, training and development and performance evaluation programs. Though the elements of those programs may appear incongruent, patterns in the practices can be discerned for certain competitive business strategies.

Small business is a very vibrant segment of the U.S. economy. Although there is a great deal of controversy as to its job-generating capabilities[16], the fact is that small business is now a viable choice of employment for many groups including women, down-sized employees and entrepreneurs. As such, understanding the operations of the small business is important to realizing its full economic contributions.

Along the same lines, a tremendous number of misconceptions exist regarding the nature of small business. Practitioners have few means by which to discern the manner in which their counterparts are conducting their businesses. Recent Requests for Proposals (RFPs) by the Small Business Administration[17] suggest that practitioners are simply not aware of the specific kinds of human resource programming other small business owners are utilizing, or the options available to them. This study is one means of providing this most basic of operating information.

Further, given the dearth of information on small business and the lack of a developing theoretical base in the area, a corporate-based model of strategy and performance is utilized. The findings of this study echo the comments of Gartner (1989), "small business is not 'little big business'"[18]. While the corporate model is a desirable starting point given a weak theoretical basis in the field, it is inadequate to explain the relationships between factors within the small business. Researchers in the field must make a concerted effort to begin formulating the foundations of such a theory for small business in order to advance the field and enhance the performance of the individual firm.

A first step in this direction would be an assessment of the competitive business strategies pursued by small businesses. As the results of this study indicate, Porter's (1980) typology of business strategy needs to be refined to address the needs of small business researchers. As mentioned earlier, interview data indicates that differentiation on a variety of factors is a clear focus of many small business owners' efforts. The owner of an Italian restaurant in discussing his conception of "quality" as a differentiating strategy, mentioned the term in conjunction with the price of items on the menu, the dress code required of diners, the tastiness of the food and the overall formality of the decor. As such, the terms used in a corporate setting needed to be further delineated for a small business setting.

The strategic management area was seen as the starting point for development of such a model in the small business area. This study utilized the concepts of strategy formulation and implementation from the strategic management model performed under conditions of rational, comprehensive decision making. Both the research project's model and questionnaire were developed based on a distinction of the two processes within the small business. The lack of clear differentiation of human resource priorities however, lends more credibility to the incremental mode of decision making. Human resource priorities exist, but as the interview data suggests, they are usually discerned in retrospect. In short, the theoretical underpinnings of small business require a great deal more investigation.

The fact that the majority of significant differences in human resource programming were found in relation to the gender of the business owner suggests the importance of gender in the small business arena. Hisrich & Brush (1983) noted that all knowledge of the entrepreneur was based upon that gained from male entrepreneurs. The need to clearly distinguish the gender of the business owner when assessing the business and its functions is apparent so that important differences in male versus female-owned businesses may be discerned. Identification of the differences and their impact on performance may lead to certain public policy decisions discussed below.

Public Policy

Affirmative action programming has received extensive attention in recent months generally focused on the equity of such programming as well as its need. Whether women's programming is included in this affirmative action category has also been in dispute. Accordingly, the recent legislative decision to set aside 5% of all government procurement programs specifically for women-owned businesses has also been called into question. The fact that clear differences exist in the manner in which women operate their businesses and the way men operate theirs suggests that further study needs to be undertaken to ascertain the impact of such differences. If the differences favorably impact the economic performance of a woman-owned firm, they ultimately impact the performance of the U.S. economy. To champion those differences and "level the playing field" the existence of such groups as the Office of Women's Business Ownership in the Small Business Administration is substantiated as is all the gender specific programming it advocates. In short, the taxpayer has some information as to whether his tax dollars have been properly spent.

Clear differences between the practices of male and female-owned firms also suggest directions for future curriculum development particularly in the business education area. Today's marketplace is much more global in its orientation than that of just a few years ago. The manner in which a firm competes in this global marketplace can be vastly different than the way it formerly competed. For example, networking, often viewed as a female asset[19], is seen as a very favorable technique to utilize in global competition. To the extent that women-owned businesses have programmatic elements that incorporate networking, the techniques utilized may need to be examined and developed into appropriate curriculum for use in the business school.

The lack of women in the low cost area is an enigma. Whether women do not pursue such a strategy due to lack of ability or a simple desire to compete on some other basis is unclear. A study concentrated in one industry where low cost strategies are prevalent would suggest whether the choice of competitive business strategy is related to gender.

Statistical and methodological limitations aside, this study has begun to identify key issues in the management of small businesses. While the corporate model of competitive business strategy and human resource management served as a viable starting point, the results of this research suggest they simply do not capture the richness of small business management. A theory of small business management needs to be developed which includes issues investigated here.

That is, any model of small business management must recognize the impact of owner characteristics such as gender. The richness and variety of small business competitive strategies must also be incorporated. Finally, the functional areas of the small business must be investigated (such as human resources, marketing, and finance), for it is in the day to day decisions that the true essence of the business can be assessed.

Small business ownership is an economic reality for many Americans and their numbers increase daily. Acquiring a better understanding of this critical part of the U.S. economy is vital to its continued expansion. This study has provided an information base for such growth.

NOTES

1. See Note # 5 of Chapter 1 Introduction of this book for a detailed discussion of the interviews held. Appendix 1 features the structured questionnaire used during the interviews.

2. The procedure utilized by the researcher in classifying firms as to their procedural or policy oriented nature is shown in Appendix 4.

3. Extensive pre-testing of the questionnaire was undertaken to determine the nature of the questions to be asked as well as the most appropriate wording for each question.

4. For a discussion of how human capital theory can be applied in the modern labor market, see Ehrenberg and Smith (1982), p. 256-269.

5. Perceptions of business owners as per questionnaire study of The National Education Center for Women in Business.

6. See Robinson and Sexton (1994).

7. Brush (1995) offers the most comprehensive review on the nature of women in small business to date.

8. From *The State of Small Business, 1994.*

9. Michael Porter's (1980) framework feature three generic competitive business strategies: overall low cost leadership, differentiation and focus.

10. Bates (1995) and Chaganti and Schneer (1994) describe various types of experience that impacts the choice of business by an individual.

11. Ostgaard and Birley (1994) note the impact of experience on the type of strategy chosen by the firm.

12. See Robinson and Sexton (1994) for the impact of experience on the success of the firm.

13. Experience also has an impact on the programming used in a firm according to a study by Neiswander, Bird and Young (1987).

14. A certified woman-owned business receives that accreditation from the Pennsylvania Equal Employment Opportunity Commission. It is a governmental effort that comes from the recognition that women have been economically disadvantaged in the past.

15. Guth and Taguiri (1965)

16. Birch (1979) and Medoff (1990) have written two decidedly disparate articles on the job generating capabilities of small business in the U.S. economy.

17. A recent Request for Proposal (RFP) issues by the Small Business Administration called for the human resource practices in the 100 best small companies in America.

18. See Gartner (1989) for a fuller discussion of this issue.

19. See Rosener (1990) for a thorough discussion of networking in female-owned businesses.

Figures

Figure 1.1: Geographic Distribution of Firms
Small Business Development Responses*

State	Number SBD	SBA Region **	Questionnai Mailed	Number Returne	Number Usable
Maine	1	I	3	1	0
Kentucky	1	IV	5	3	3
California	2	IX	8	4	3
Pennsylvania	8	III	50	37	25
Wisconsin	1	V	6	6	6
Ohio	1	V	10	8	8
Nevada	1	IX	10	8	8
Alabama	1	IV	3	1	1
New York	1	II	10	6	6
Washington	1	X	3	3	3
Michigan	1	V	5	4	4
Colorado	1	VIII	10	5	5
Illinois	1	V	5	4	4
Georgia	1	IV	5	3	3
Delaware	1	III	4	1	1
Missouri	1	VII	3	3	3
Texas	1	VI	5	2	0
Maryland	1	III	10	0***	0
Total			155	95	83

*   Two SBDCs requested that their names not be published for client
     confidentiality purposes. Accordingly, all information is aggregated and
     presented on an SBA region basis by state.
**   SBA Regions: See Note 1
***   Communication with Maryland SBDC suggests that all ten questionnaires
     were completed and mailed. However, they were never received.

Figure 1.2: Lines of Businesses Represented in Study Sample
(Number in parenthesis represents number of firms in each line of business.)

Agricultural Products (8)	Industrial Sales (5)
Appliances (1)	Instrumentation (3)
Automotive Parts (3)	Leisure Time (3)
Automotive Sales (4)	Materials Handling (2)
Banking Services (1)	Metals and Mining (4)
Beverages (2)	Natural Resources (2)
Building Materials (2)	Office Equipment (8)
Chemicals (2)	Oil Service and Supply (2)
Communication Arts (13)	Paper and Forest Products (6)
Construction (8)	Personal Care Products (4)
Construction Services (2)	Publishing (3)
Containers (2)	Research and Development (4)
Electrical, Electronics (5)	Retailing-Food (5)
Food Processing (9)	Retailing-Nonfood (8)
General Manufacturing (10)	Special Machinery (10)
General Machinery (8)	Steel (5)
General Service Industries (37)	Textiles, Apparel (6)
Health Care (6)	Trucking (2)
Health Care Product Sales (6)	

Figure 2.1: Human Resource Strategy Definitions and Perspectives

Business Human Resource Strategy: A pattern of human resource priorities within an organization.

Functional Human Resource Strategy: A pattern of human resource programs, policies and plans implemented by a human resource department.

Issue	Study Orientation	Model/Definition Focus
Content vs. Process	Content	Decisions on priorities (BHRS)
	Process	Decisions on programs, policies and plans (FHRS)
Incremental vs. Rational	Rational	Decisions on priorities (BHRS)
	Incremental	Decisions on programs, plans and policies (FHRS)
Intended vs. Realized	Intended	Decisions on priorities
	Realized	Programs, plans, policies enacted
Level	Business Unit	Decisions on human resources for the firm
	Functional	Decisions on programs in the Human Resource Department
Scope	Goals	Priorities are the goals for human resources in the firm
	Means	Programs are the means of attaining human resource priorities

Figure 2.2: Human Resource Priorities: Examples

Short Term Focus	Long Term Focus
Predictable, repetitive task approach	Creative, innovative task approach
Independent, individual behavior	Cooperative, group based behavior
Process orientation	Results orientation

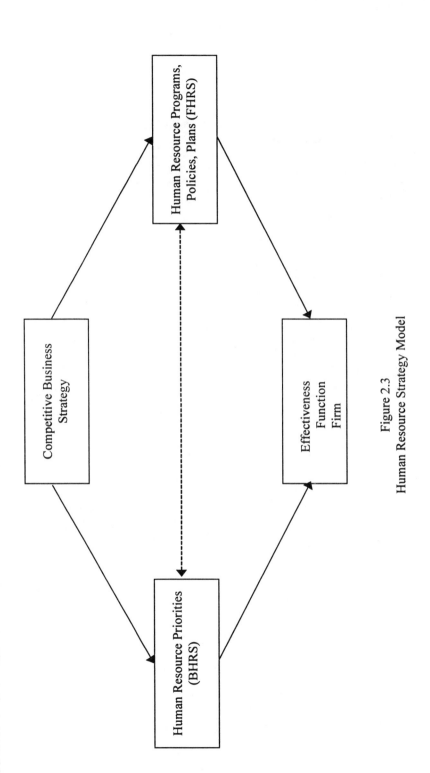

Figure 2.3
Human Resource Strategy Model

Figure 3.1: Anticipated Pattern in Human Resource Priorities by Competitive Business Strategy

Low Cost	Differentiation
Short term focus	Long term focus
Constant, predictable approach	Creative, innovative approach
Independent behavior	Cooperative behavior
Single task focus	Job flexibility
Concern with rules, procedures	Concern with outcomes
Limited personal responsibility	Major personal responsibility
Major commitment to job	Major commitment to organization
Heavy efficiency focus	Minimal efficiency focus

**Figure 4.1: Assessment of Programming Across Functions:
Differentiation Profile**

Programmatic Element	Policy/ Procedure	Individual/ Group	Firm specific/ General
Contributions to firm impact pay	Policy	Individual	Firm Specific
Pay based on individual achievement	Policy	Individual	Firm Specific
Job-based pay	Policy	Group	Firm Specific
Long term focus rewarded	Policy	Individual	Firm Specific
Pay based on group achievement	Policy	Group	Firm Specific
Pay information secret in firm	Policy	Group	General
Skill-based pay	Policy	Individual	Firm Specific
Personality Tests	Procedure	Group	General
Honesty Tests	Procedure	Group	General
Personal referrals	Procedure	Individual	Firm Specific
Job fairs	Procedure	Group	General
Electronic Bulletin Boards	Procedure	Group	General
Networking	Procedure	Individual	Firm Specific
Walk-ins	Procedure	Individual	Firm Specific
Written job descriptions on file	Policy	Group	Firm Specific
Skills kept on file	Policy	Individual	Firm Specific
Lectures	Procedure	Group	General

Figure 4.1 (continued)

Videotapes	Procedure	Group	General
Computer-aided instruction	Procedure	Individual	General
Role playing	Procedure	Individual	General
Oral communication skills	Procedure	Group	General
Decision making skills	Procedure	Group	General
Group dynamics skills	Procedure	Group	General
Firm has formal written PA	Policy	Group	Firm Specific
Results used for training	Policy	Individual	Firm Specific
Results used for performance improvement	Policy	Individual	Firm Specific
Employees help determine standards.	Policy	Individual	Firm Specific
Self evaluation	Policy	Individual	Firm Specific
Employee Handbooks	Procedure	Group	General
Newsletters	Procedure	Group	General
Internal Memos	Procedure	Group	Firm Specific
Suggestion Systems	Procedure	Group	Firm Specific

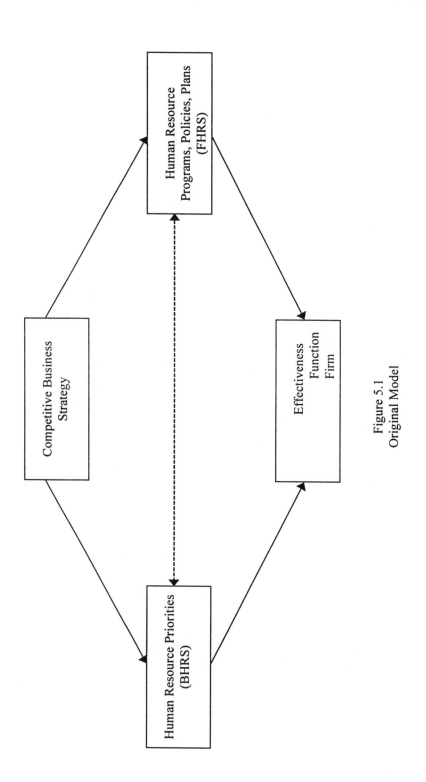

Figure 5.1
Original Model

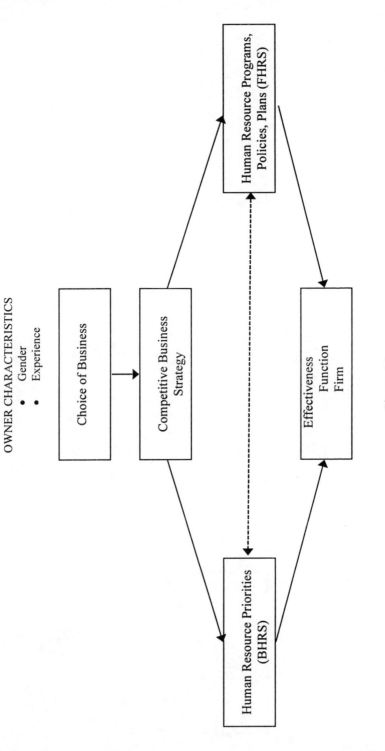

OWNER CHARACTERISTICS
- Gender
- Experience

Choice of Business

Competitive Business Strategy

Human Resource Programs, Policies, Plans (FHRS)

Human Resource Priorities (BHRS)

Effectiveness Function Firm

Figure 5.2
Revised Model

Appendices

APPENDIX 1: SEMI-STRUCTURED INTERVIEW WITH ENTREPRENEUR

Part One: Demographic Information

Company Name:

In what industry does your firm operate?

Describe the products/services your firm produces.

What is the geographic scope of each of these products/services?

Probes (if needed):
local, regional, national, international (product/service associated with associated with each and/or percentage of product/service allocated by geographic region)

What is the location of your main place of business? Any "satellite" locations?

In what year was this business started? Dates of expansion (planned or realized).

How many employees do you have at each plant/office location? What is the breakdown of those employees by job type/classification?

(Probes):
Executive and Managerial; supervisory; technical; professional; clerical; sales; and production and maintenance.

Part Two: Entrepreneur Characteristics

Sex

Age

Tell me about your educational background.

(Probes):
> High school (college preparatory/vocational/technical curriculum);
> Institutions/Degree(s)/Major/Minor
> Additional Training (certificates); non-degree courses; seminars)

Tell me about your work experience

(Probes):
> Previous jobs/dates/firms/duties
> Association memberships/affiliations

Part Three: Business Strategy

Why would I buy your product over your competitors?

(Probes):
> Quality, price, uniqueness

(Alternate wording):
> What differentiates your firm from its competitors?

Part Four: Human Resource Priorities

What are the factors you see as important in having your employees
succeed at their jobs (this may be broken down by job category)?

(Alternate wording):
> What do you have to get out of your employees in order for your
> firm to compete? (Again this may be broken down into job
> categories).

(As an additional probe and for a reliability check, the following
"Questionnaire" will be given to the entrepreneur):

The following items describe factors managers have considered
important for employees to exhibit to successfully complete their jobs.

Examples of each factor are provided. Indicate the degree of importance of the factor to your organization using the following scale.

1:	Not important at all:	This factor is of no concern to my organization
2:	Somewhat important:	This factor is a concern, but it has low priority.
3:	Important:	This factor is a concern and I consider it to have an impact on job completion.
4:	Very important:	This factor has high priority and is necessary to job completion.
5:	Vital:	This factor has top priority. It is key to completing the job.

Labor cost control:	Keeping a tight rein on costs through use of a piece rate system, for example	1 2 3 4 5
Employee skill flexibility:	Workers can rotate between jobs	1 2 3 4 5
Employee mobility:	Workers move readily between jobs	1 2 3 4 5
Employee responsibility:	Workers participate in decision making	1 2 3 4 5
Job security:	A no layoff policy is in place	1 2 3 4 5
Employee motivation:	A profit sharing plan is available to workers	1 2 3 4 5
Consistent employee productivity:	A program is in place in the firm which rewards workers who are not absent	1 2 3 4 5
Employee development:	Training seminars are provided to employees	1 2 3 4 5
Employee innovation:	A quality circle program is in place in the firm	1 2 3 4 5
Employee initiative:	A group gainsharing program is in place in the firm	1 2 3 4 5
Employee competencies:	There is a broad skill mix in the firm	1 2 3 4 5

(Further probes):

> Do your workers perform repetitive or creative tasks?
>
> Are workers' jobs short term or long term in orientation?
>
> Do workers' perform jobs independent of one another or does one job directly depend on the next?
>
> Is quality stressed?
>
> Is a quota established for this?
>
> Does the worker take risks in his job or must he avoid risks?
>
> Is the process of the job stressed (i.e. completing each step in the job) or is the concern with getting the product out?
>
> Does the worker assume any type of responsibility in his job?
>
> If a change occurs in some aspect of the job, does the worker have some flexibility in dealing with that change?
>
> Does the worker need a narrow or a broad skill range to complete his job?
>
> Is the worker highly involved in his job?

Part Five: Internal Environmental Factors

Values:	Weber's (1988) abbreviated Rokeach survey is given to the entrepreneur
Managerial Style:	Would you classify yourself as principally a task oriented manager or people oriented manager? Why?
(Alternate Probe):	Here are two descriptions of managers. Which most closely matches the way in which you manager? (The descriptions to be provided will contain characteristics of the task oriented manager versus the people oriented one.)

Part Six: External Environmental Factors

External Labor Markets:
Unemployment rate (area)
Quit rate

Union Presence:
Is your firm unionized?
Union affiliation?
Which workers are unionized?

**APPENDIX 2: CONTENT ANALYSIS FORMAT: INTERVIEW
TRANSCRIPTS**

Human Resource Priority Addressed
  Terminology Used
  Frequency of Use
  Relative Percentage of Discussion Focused on

Human Resource Activity/Program Addressed
  Scope of Activity   Terminology Used
  Focus of Activity   Frequency of Usage
  Time Horizon of Activity   Relative Percentage of Discussion
                             Focused on

APPENDIX 3: CONTENT ANALYSIS FORMAT: COMPANY DOCUMENTS

Human Resource Activity/Program Addressed
Scope of Activity
Focus of Activity
Time Horizon of Activity
Terminology Used

APPENDIX 4: DEFINITIONS OF PROGRAMMING ASSESSMENT

A researcher developed technique was utilized to assess the human resource programming elements of this study. The technique was designed to ascertain patterns in the elements for a better understanding of the nature of decisions made under each competitive business strategy.

Programming elements were assessed on the following basis:

1. Policy: The manner in which data is utilized in decision making; a guideline to decision making; versus
2. Procedure: The technique used to acquire data about an employee.
3. Individual: Information has the individual as its primary focus; versus
4. Group: Information has the group as the primary focus.
5. Firm Specific: Outcomes principally used within the firm. versus

   General: Outcomes used as readily outside as inside firm.

Bibliography

Alpander, G. and Botter, C. "An Integrated Model of Strategic Human Resource Planning and Utilization." *Human Resource Planning*, 1981, 189-203.

Amba-Rao, S. and Pendse, D. "Human Resource Compensation and Maintenance Practices." *American Journal of Small Business*, 1985, 10(2), 19-29.

Anderson, C.R. and Zeithaml, C.P. "Stage of the Product Life Cycle, Business Strategy, and Business Performance." *Academy of Management Journal*, 1984, 27(1), 5-14.

Andrews, K. R. *The Concept of Corporate Strategy*. Homewood, Ill.: Irwin, 1971.

Ansoff, I. H., Avner, J., Brandenburg, R. G., Portner, E. F., and Radosevich, R. "Does Planning Pay? The Effect of Planning on Success and Acquisition in American Firms." *Long Range Planning*, December, 1970, 3(2), 2-8.

Arthur, J. "The Link Between Business Strategy and Industrial Relations Systems in American Steel Minimills." *Industrial and Labor Relations Review*, April, 1992, 45(3), 488-506.

Baker, H. and Feldman, D. "Linking Organizational Socialization Tactics with Corporate Human Resource Management Strategies." *Human Resource Management Review,* 1991, 1(3), 193-202.

Balkin, D. and Gomez-Mejia, L. "Matching Compensation and Organizational Strategies." *Strategic Management Journal*, 1990, 11, 153-169.

Balkin, D. and Gomez-Mejia, L. "Toward a Contingency Theory of Compensation Strategy." *Strategic Management Journal*, 1987, 8, 169-182.

Ballentine, J.W., Cleveland, F.W., and Koeller, C. T. "Characterizing Profitable and Unprofitable Strategies in Small and Large Businesses." *Journal of Small Business Management*, April, 1992, 13-23.

149

Bamberger, P., Dyer, L., and Bacharach, S. "Human Resource Planning in High Technology Entrepreneurial Startups." *Human Resource Planning*, 1990, 13, 37-44.

Bamberger, P. and Phillips, B. "Organizational Environment and Business Strategy: Parallel Versus Conflicting Influencees on Human Resource Strategy in the Pharmaceutical Industry." *Human Resource Management*, 1991, 30, 153-182.

Bates, T. "Self-employment Entry Across Industry Groups." *Journal of Business Venturing*, 1995, 10, 143-156.

Birch, D. *Job Creation in America: How Our Smallest Companies Put the Most People to Work.* Detroit: The Free Press, 1987.

Blake, R. and Mouton, J.S. *The Managerial Grid.* Houston: Gulf Publishing, 1964.

Boeker, W. "Strategic Change: The Effects of Founding and History." *Academy of Management Journal*, 1989, 32(3), 489-515.

Boeker, W. "Strategic Origins: Entrepreneurial and Environmental Imprinting at Founding." *Academy of Management Proceedings—Best Papers*, New Orleans, 1987, p. 150-153.

Boudreau, J. and Berman, R. "Using Performance Measurement to Evaluate Strategic Human Resource Management Decisions: Kodak's Experience with Profit-Sharing." *Human Resource Management*, Fall 1991, 30(3), 393-410.

Bourgeois, L.J. "Strategy and Environment: A Conceptual Integration." *Academy of Management Review*, 1980, 5, 25-39.

Bowen, D.D. and Hisrich, R.D. "The Female Entrepreneur: A Career Development Perspective." *Academy of Management Review*, 1986, 11(2), 393-407.

Box, T., Watts, L. and Hisrich, R. "Manufacturing Entrepreneurs: An Empirical Study of the Correlates of Employment Growth in the Tulsa MSA and Rural East Texas." *Journal of Business Venturing*, 1994, 9, 261-270.

Broderick, R. "Pay Policy and Business Strategy: Toward a Measure of "Fit". In Milkovich, G. "A Strategic Perspective on Compensation Management." In *Research in Personnel and Human Resources Management*, 1988, 3, 263-288.

Broom, H. and Longenecker, J. *Small Business Management.* Cincinnati, OH: Southwestern Publishing Company, 1975.

Brush, C. "Research on Women Business Owners: Past Trends, A New Perspective and Future Directions." *Entrepreneurship Theory and Practice*, Summer, 1992, 5-31.

Brush, C. "Women's Management Styles and Strategies: A Literature Review." working paper, National Education Center for Women in Business, 1993.

Brush, C. G. "Women-Owned Businesses: The State of Our Knowledge and Issues for the Future." working paper, Boston University, 1994.

Buller, P., Beck-Dudley, C., and McEvoy, G. "Competitive Strategy and Human Resource Practices in a Professional Service Environment." *Human Resource Planning*, 1990, 13(1), 27-36.

Burns, T. and Stalker, G. *The Management of Innovation*. London: Tavistock, 1961.

Butler, J., Ferris, G., and Napier, N. "Entrepreneurial Links." In *Strategy and Human Resource Management*, Cincinnati, Ohio: Southwestern Publishing, 1991.

Bygrave, W. and Hofer, C. "Theorizing about Entrepreneurship." *Entrepreneurship Theory and Practice*, Winter, 1991, 13-22.

Byrne, John A., Introduction to "Enterprise: How Entrepreneurs are Reshaping the Economy -and What Big Companies Can Learn." *Business Week*, 1993.

Camillus, J. and Venkatraman, N. "Dimensions of Strategic Choice." *Planning Review*, January, 1994, 26-32.

Carney, T.F. *Content Analysis: A Technique for Systematic Inference from Communication*. Winnipeg, Canada: University of Manitoba Press, 1972.

Carroll, S. "Business Strategies and Compensation Systems." In *New Perspectives on Compensation*. Balkin, D. and Gomez-Mejia, L. (eds.). Englewood Cliffs, N.J: Prentice-Hall, 1987.

Carter, N., Stearns, T.M., Reynolds, P.D., and Miller, B. A. "New Venture Strategies: Theory Development with an Empirical Base." *Strategic Management Journal*, 1994, 15(1), 21-41.

Certo, S. and Peter, J.P. *Strategic Management: Concepts and Applications*. New York, N.Y.: McGraw-Hill, Inc., 1991.

Chaffee, E. "Three Models of Strategy." *Academy of Management Review*, 1985, 10(1), 89-96.

Chaganti, R., "Small Business Strategies in Different Industry Growth Environments." *Journal of Small Business Management*, July, 1987, 25(3), 61-68.

Chaganti, R., Chaganti, R., and Mahajan, V. "Profitable Small Business Strategies Under Different Types of Competition." *Entrepreneurship Theory and Practice*, Spring, 1989, 21-35.

Chaganti, R. and Schneer, J. "A Study of the Impact of Owner's Mode of Entry on Venture Performance and Management Patterns." *Journal of Business Venturing*, 1994, 9, 243-260.

Chandler, A. D. *Strategy and Structure: Chapters in the History of American Enterprise*. Cambridge, MA.: MIT Press, 1962.

Chandler, G. and Hanks, S. "Measuring the Performance of Emerging Businesses: A Validation Study." *Journal of Business Venturing*, 1993, 8, 391-408.

Cicco, J., December 19, 1993 interview with researcher.

Cook, D. and Ferris, G. "Strategic Human Resource Management and Firm Effectiveness in Industries Experiencing Decline." *Human Resource Management*, Fall, 1986, 25(3), 441-458.

Cooper, A., Gimeno-Gascon, F. and Woo, C. "Initial Human and Financial Capital as Predictors of New Venture Performance." *Journal of Business Venturing*, 1994, 9, 371-395.

Covin, J. "Entrepreneurial Versus Conservative Firms: A Comparison of Strategies and Performance." *Journal of Management Studies*, 1991, 28, 439-462.

Covin, J. and Covin, T. "Competitive Aggressiveness, Environmental Context, and Small Firm Performance." *Entrepreneurship Theory and Practice*, Summer, 1990, 35-50.

Covin, J. and Prescott, J. "Strategies, Styles and Structures of Small Product Innovative Firms in High and Low Technology Industries." working paper, University of Pittsburgh 1989.

Covin, J. and Slevin, D. "The Development and Testing of an Organizational-Level Entrepreneurship Scale." *Frontiers of Entrepreneurship Research*, Babson College, 1986, 628-639.

Covin, J. and Slevin, D. "The Influence of Organization Structure on the Utility of an Entrepreneurial Top Management Style." *Journal of Management Studies*, 1988a, 25, 217-234.

Covin, J. and Slevin, D. "New Venture Competitive Strategy: An Industry Life Cycle Analysis." *Frontiers of Entrepreneurship Research*, Babson College, 1988b, 446-459.

Covin, J. and Slevin, D. "A Conceptual Model of Entrepreneurship as Firm Behavior." *Entrepreneurship Theory and Practice*, Fall, 1991, 16(1), 7-25.

Craft, J. "A Critical Perspective on Human Resource Planning." working paper, University of Pittsburgh, 1980.

Craft, J. "Human Resource Planning: Its Roots, Identity and Development in Management Thought." working paper, University of Pittsburgh, 1990.

Craft, J. "Human Resource Planning and Strategy." working paper, University of Pittsburgh, 1987.

Craft, J. "Human Resources Planning and Strategy." In L. Dyer (ed.), *Human Resource Management: Evolving Roles and Responsibilities.* Washington, D.C.: BNA Series, 1988, Chapter 2.

Cragg, P. and King, M. "Organizational Characteristics and Small Firms' Performance Revisited." *Entrepreneurship Theory and Practice,* 1988, 13(2), 49-64.

Davidson, W. and Dutia, D. "Debt, Liquidity, and Profitability Problems in Small Firms." *Entrepreneurship Theory and Practice,* Fall, 1991, 53-64.

De Bejar, G. and Milkovich, G. "Human Resource Strategy at the Business Level: Study 1: Theoretical Model and Empirical Verification." Paper presented at Academy of Management Meetings, Chicago, 1986a.

De Bejar, G. and Milkovich, G. "Human Resource Strategy at the Business Level: Study 2: Relationship between Strategy and Performance Components." Paper presented at Academy of Management Meetings, Chicago, 1986b.

Deshpande, S. and Golhar, D. "HRM Practices in Large and Small Manufacturing Firms: A Comparative Study." *Journal of Small Business Management,* 1994, 49-56.

Dess, G. and Davis, P. "Porter's (1980) Generic Strategies as Determinants of Strategic Group Membership and Organizational Performance." *Academy of Management Journal,* 1984, 27(3), 467-488.

Dess, G and Robinson, R. "Measuring Organizational Performance in the Absence of Objective Measures: The Case of the Privately-held Firm and Conglomerate Business Unit." *Strategic Management Journal,* 1984, 5, 265-273.

Dubini, P. "The Influence of Motivations and Environment on Business Start-ups: Some Hints for Public Policies." *Journal of Business Venturing,* 1988, 4, 11-26.

Duchesneau, D. and Gartner, W. "A Profile of New Venture Success and Failure in an Emerging Industry." *Journal of Business Venturing,* 1989, 5, 297-312.

Dunkelberg, W. and Cooper, A "Entrepreneurial Typologies: An Empirical Study." *Frontiers of Entrepreneurship Research,* Babson College, 1982, 1-15.

Dyer, L. "Bringing Human Resources into the Strategy Formulation Process." working paper, Cornell University, 1983.

Dyer, L. "Strategic Human Resources Management and Planning." In *Research in Personnel and Human Resources Management*, Eds. Rowland, K. M. and Ferris, G. R., Greenwich, CT: JAI Press Inc., 1985, 3, 1-30.

Dyer, L. "Studying Human Resource Strategy: An Approach and an Agenda." *Industrial Relations*, 1984, 23(2), 156-169.

Dyer, L. and Holder, G. "A Strategic Perspective of Human Resource Management." In L. Dyer (ed.) *Human Resource Management: Evolving Roles and Responsibilities*. Washington, D.C.: BNA Series, 1988, Chapter 1.

Fagenson, E. "Personal Value Sytems of Men and Women Entrepreneurs versus Managers." *Journal of Business Venturing*, 1993, 8, 409-430.

Feeser, H. and Williard, G. "Founding Strategy and Performance: A Comparison of High and Low Growth Tech Firms." *Strategic Management Journal*, 1990 11, 87-98.

Ferris, G., Russ, G., Albanese, R., and Martocchio, J. "Personnel/Human Resources Management, Unionization, and Strategy Determinants of Organizational Performance." *Human Resource Planning*, 1990, 13(3), 215-227.

Ferris, G., Schellenberg, D. and Zammuto, R. "Human Resource Management Strategies in Declining Industries." *Human Resource Management*, 1984, 23, 381-394.

Filley, A. and Aldag, R. "Characteristics and Measurement of an Organizational Typology." *Academy of Management Journal*, 1978, 21(4), 578-591.

Fiorito, J. "The Rationale for Human Resource Planning." *Human Resource Planning*, 1982, 103-107.

Fisher, C. "Current and Recurrent Challenges in HRM." *Journal of Management*, 1989, 15, 157-180.

Fischer, E., Reuber, A., and Dyke, L. "A Theoretical Overview and Extension of Research on Sex, Gender and Entrepreneurship." *Journal of Business Venturing*, 1991, 8, 151-168.

Fombrun, C., Tichy, N. and Devanna, M. *Strategic Human Resource Management*. New York: John Wiley & Sons, Inc., 1984.

Fombrun, C.J. and Wally, S. "Structuring Small Firms for Rapid Growth." *Journal of Business Venturing*, 1989, 4(2), 107-122.

Freeman, R. and Medoff, J. *What Do Unions Do*? New York: Basic Books, 1984.

Gable, M. and Topol, M. "Planning Practices of Small Scale Retailers." *American Journal of Small Business*, Fall, 1987, 12(2), 19-32.

Galbraith, J. and Nathanson, D. *Strategy Implementation: The Role of Structure and Process*. St. Paul, MN: West Publishing, 1978.

Gartner, W. "A Conceptual Framework for Describing the Phenonmenon of New Venture Creation." *Academy of Management Review*, 1985, 10(4), 696-706.

Gartner, W. "Some Suggestions for Research on Entrepreneurial Traits and Characteristics." *Entrepreneurship Theory and Practice*, 1989, 27-37.

Gartner, W. "What are We Talking about When We Talk about Entrepreneurship?" *Journal of Business Venturing*, 1990, 5, 15-28.

Gartner, W. "'Who Is an Entrepreneur?' Is the Wrong Question." *Entrepreneurship Theory and Practice*, Summer, 1989, 13(4), 47-68.

Gatewood, R. and Feild, H. "A Personnel Selection Program for Small Business." *Journal of Small Business Management*, 1987, 25(4), 16-24.

Gilligan, C. *In a Different Voice*. Cambridge, MA: Harvard University Press, 1982.

Gomez-Mejia, L. "The Role of Human Resource Strategy in Export Performance: A Longitudinal Study." *Strategic Management Journal*, 1988, 9, 493-505.

Gomez-Mejia, L. and Balkin, D. *Compensation, Organization Strategy and Firm Performance*. Cincinnati, OH: Southwestern Publishing Company, 1992.

Gould, R. "Gaining a Competitive Edge Through Human Resource Strategies." *Human Resource Planning*, 1984, 31-38.

Grant, J. and King, W. *The Logic of Strategic Planning*. Boston: Little, Brown and Company, 1982.

Grinyer, P. and Norburn, D. "Strategic Planning in 21 U.K. Companies." *Long Range Planning*, August, 1974, 7(4), 80-88.

Groe, G. "Legitimizing Human Resource Planning." *Human Resource Planning*, 1980, 11-14.

Gupta, A. "Matching Managers to Strategies: Point and Counterpoint." *Human Resource Management*, Summer, 1986, 25(2), 215-234.

Gupta, A. and Govindarajan, V. "Business Unit Strategy, Managerial Characteristics and Business Unit Effectiveness at Strategy Implementation." *Academy of Management Journal*, 1984, 27(1), 25-41.

Guth, W. and Tagiuri, R. "Personal Values and Corporate Strategy." *Harvard Business Review*, September/October, 1965, 123-132.

Guthrie, J. and Olian, J. "Does Context Affect Staffing Decisions? The Case of General Managers." *Personnel Psychology*, 1991, 44, 263-292.

Hambrick, D. "Operationalizing the Concept of Business-Level Strategy in Research." *Academy of Management Review*, 1980, 5(4), 567-575.

Hax, A. "A Methodology for the Development of a Human Resource Strategy." working paper, Sloan School of Management, MIT, 1985.

Hennig, M. and Jardim, A. *The Managerial Woman*, Garden City, NJ: Anchor Press-Doubleday, 1977.

Herold, D. "Long Range Planning and Organizational Performance: A Cross Validation Study." *Academy of Management Journal*, March, 1972, 15(1), 91-104.

Hills, S. "Organizational Politics and Human Resource Planning." *Human Resource Planning*, Spring, 1978, 31-37.

Hisrich, R. and Brush, C. "The Woman Entrepreneur: Implications of Family, Educational and Occupational Experience." *Frontiers of Entrepreneurship Research*, Babson College, 1983, 255-170.

Hisrich, R. and Brush, C. "Women and Minority Entrepreneurs: A Comparative Analysis." *Frontiers of Entrepreneurship Research*, Babson College, 1985, 566-587.

Hisrich, R. and Brush, C. *The Woman Entrepreneur: Starting, Financing, and Managing a Successful New Business*, Lexington, MA: Lexington Books, 1986.

Hisrich, R. and O'Brien, M. "The Woman Entrepreneur from a Business and Sociological Perspective." *Frontiers of Entrepreneurship Research*, Babson College, 1981, 21-39.

Hisrich, R. and O'Brien, M. "The Woman Entrepreneur as a Reflection of the Type of Business." *Frontiers of Entrepreneurship Research*, Babson College, 1982, 54-67.

Hofer, C. "Toward a Contingency Theory of Business Strategy." *Academy of Management Journal*, 1975, 18, 784-810.

Hofer, C. "Improving New Venture Performance: Some Guidelines for Success." *American Journal of Small Business*, Summer, 1987, 12(1),11-25.

Hofer, C., Bygrave, W. and Sandberg, W. "Researching Entrepreneurship." *Entrepreneurship Theory and Practice*, Spring, 1992, 91-100.

Hofer, C. and Schendel, D. *Strategy Formulation: Analytical Concepts*. St. Paul, MN: West Publishing, 1978.

Holoviak, S. and DeCenzo, D, "Effective Employee Relations: An Aid in Small Business." *American Journal of Small Business*, 1982, 6(3), 49-54.

Honig-Haftel, S. "Is the Female Entrepreneur at a Disadvantage?" *Thrust: The Journal for Employment and Training Professionals*, 1986, 7(1), 49-64.

Hornsby, J. and Kuratko, D. "Human Resource Management in Small Business: Critical Issues for the 1990's." *Journal of Small Business Management*, July, 1990, 9-18.

Huselid, M. "Human Resource Management Practices and Firm Performance." working paper, Rutgers University, 1993a.

Huselid, M. "The Impact of Human Resource Management Practices on Turnover and Productivity." working paper, Institute for Management and Labor Relations, Rutgers University, October, 1993b.

Huselid, M. "Yes, Virginia, HR Contributes to the Bottom Line." *HR Magazine*, August 1993c, 62-63.

Huselid, "Documenting HR's Effect on Company Performance." *Human Resource Magazine*, January, 1994, 79-85.

Hutchens, N. "Toward a Human Resource Planning Design Model." *Human Resource Planning*, 1980, 15-21.

Jackson, S., Schuler, R. and Rivero, J. "Organizational Characteristics as Predictors of Personnel Practices." *Personnel Psychology*, 1989, 42, 727-786.

James, R. "Effective Planning Strategies." *Human Resource Planning*, 1980, 1-10.

Jones, T. *Entrepreneurism: The Mythical, The True and the New*. NY: Donald I. Fine, Inc., 1987.

Karger, D. and Malik, Z. "Long Range Planning and Organizational Performance." *Long Range Planning*, 1975, 8(6), 60-64.

Keats, B. and Bracker, J. "Toward a Theory of Small Firms Performance: A Conceptual Model." *American Journal of Small Business*, 1988, 12(4),41-58.

Kelleher, E. and Cotter, K. "An Integrative Model for Human Resource Planning and Strategic Planning." *Human Resource Planning*, 1982, 15-22.

Kerr, J. "Diversification Strategies and Managerial Rewards: An Empirical Study." *Academy of Management Journal*, 1985, 28(1), 155-179.

King, W. "Evaluating Strategic Planning Systems." *Strategic Management Journal*, 1983, 263-277.

Kochan, T., McKersie, R. and Cappelli, P. "Strategic Choices and Industrial Relations Theory." *Industrial Relations*, 1984, 23, 16-39.

Kudla, R. "The Effects of Strategic Planning on Common Stock Returns." *Academy of Management Journal*, 1980, 23(1), 5-20.

Kuehl, C. and Lambing, P. *Small Business: Planning and Management*. Orlando, FL: The Dryden Press, 1990.

LaBelle, C. 1983. "Human Resources Strategic Decisions as Responses to Environmental Challenges." In Dyer, L. "Strategic Human Resources Management and Planning," In *Research in Personnel and Human Resources Management*, Eds. Rowland, K. and Ferris, G., 1985, 1-30.

Lawrence, P. and Lorsch, H. *Organization and Environment: Managing Differentiation and Integration*. Homewood, IL: Richard D. Irwin, Inc., 1969.

Lenz, R. "Determinants of Organizational Performance: An Interdisciplinary Review." *Strategic Management Journal*, 1981, 2, 131-154.

Lewis, H. *Unionism and Relative Wages in the United States*. Chicago: University of Chicago Press, 1963.

Lorange, P. and Vancil, R. *Strategic Planning Systems*. Englewood Cliffs, N.J.: Prentice-Hall, 1977.

Lyles, M., Baird, I., Orris J., and Kuratko, D. "Formalized Planning in Small Business: Increasing Strategic Choices." *Journal of Small Business Management*, April 1993, 38-50.

McDougall, P. and Robinson, R. "New Venture Performance: Patterns of Strategic Behavior in Different Industries." *Frontiers of Entrepreneurship Research*, Babson College, 1988, 477-491.

McDougall, P. and Robinson, R. "New Venture Strategies: An Empirical Identification of Eight 'Archetypes' of Competitive Strategies for Entry." *Strategic Management Journal*, 1990, 11(6), 447-467.

McEvoy, G. "Personnel Practices in Smaller Firms: A Survey and Recommendations." *Journal of Small Business Management*, 1984, 1-8.

Miles, R. "Human Relations of Human Resources." *Harvard Business Review*, July/August, 1965, 148-163.

Miles, R. and Snow, C. *Organizational Strategy, Structure and Process*. New York: McGraw-Hill, 1978.

Miles, R. and Snow, C. "Designing Strategic Human Resources Systems." *Organizational Dynamics*, 1984, 36-52.

Miles, R., Snow, C., Meyer, A. and Coleman, H. "Organizational Strategy, Structure, and Process." *Academy of Management Review*, July, 1978, 546-562.

Milkovich, G. "A Strategic Perspective on Compensation Management," In *Research in Personnel and Human Resource Management*. Eds. Rowland, K. and Ferris, G. 1988, 263-288.

Miller, D. and Toulouse, J. "Strategy, Structure, CEO Personality and Performance in Small Firms." *American Journal of Small Business*, 1986, 10(3), 47-62.

Mintzberg, H. "Patterns in Strategy Formation." *Management Science*, 1978, 934-948.

Mintzberg, H. "Strategy-Making in Three Modes." *California Management Review*, 1973, 16(2), 44-53.

Mintzberg, H. and Waters, J. "Of Strategies, Deliberate and Emergent." *Strategic Management Journal*, 1985, 6, 257-272.

Moates, W. and Kulonda, D. "An Examination of Differences Between Supervisors in Large and Small Companies." *Journal of Small Business Management*, July, 1990, 27-36.

Moore, D., Buttner, E., and Rosen, B. "Stepping Off the Corporate Track: The Entrepreneurial Alternative." In *Womanpower: Managing in Times of Demographic Turbulence*. Eds. Sekaran U. and Leong, F. T., Newbury Park, CA: Sage Publications, 1992, 85-110.

Mosakowski, E. "A Resource-Based Perspective on The Dynamic Strategy-Performance Relationship: An Empirical Examination of the Focus and Differentiation Strategies in Entrepreneurial Firms." *Journal of Management*, 1993, 19(4), 819-839.

Naman, J. and Slevin, D. "Entrepreneurship and the Concept of Fit: A Model and Empirical Tests." *Strategic Management Journal*, 1993, 14, 137-153.

National Foundation of Women Business Owners (NFWBO). "Styles of Success: The Thinking and Management Styles of Women and Men Entrepreneurs." Washington, D.C.: The National Foundation for Women Business Owners, 1994.

National Foundation of Women Business Owners (NFWBO). "Breaking the Boundaries: The Progress and Achievement of Women-Owned Enterprises." Washington, D.C.: The National Foundation for Women Business Owners, 1995.

Neiswander, K., Bird, B., and Young, P. "Entrepreneurial Hiring and Management of Early Stage Employees." *Frontiers of Entrepreneurship Research*, Babson College, 1987, 204-219.

Newman, J. "Selecting Incentive Plans to Complement Organizational Strategy." In *New Perspectives on Compensation*. Balkin, D. and Gomez-Mejia, L. (eds.). Englewood Cliffs, N.J: Prentice-Hall, 1987.

Newsweek, "Gray Matters." March 27, 1995, 48-54.

Nkomo, S. "Human Resource Planning and Organization Performance: An Exploratory Analysis." *Strategic Management Journal*, 1987, 8, 387-392.

Olian J. and Rynes, S. "Organizational Staffing: Integrating Practice with Strategy." *Industrial Relations*, Spring, 1984, 23(2), 170-183.

Olson, S. and Currie, H. "Female Entrepreneurs: Personal Value Systems and Business Strategies in a Male-Dominated Industry." *Journal of Small Business Management*, January, 1992, 49-57.

Ostgaard, T. and Birley, S. "Personal Networks and Firm Competitive Strategy—A Strategic or Coincidental Match?" *Journal of Business Venturing*, 1994, 9, 281-305.

Osterman, P. (ed.). *Internal Labor Markets*. Cambridge, MA: MIT Press, 1984.

Peacock, P. "The Influence of Risk Taking as a Cognitive Judgmental Behavior of Small Business Success." *Frontiers of Entrepreneurship Research*, Babson College, 1986, 110-118.

Pearce, J., Freeman, E., and Robinson, R. "The Tenuous Link Between Formal Strategic Planning and Financial Performance." *Academy of Management Review*, 1987, 12(4), 658-675.

Peters, T. and Waterman, P. *In Search of Excellence*. New York: Warner Books, 1982.

Peters, T. and Austin, N. *A Passion for Excellence*. New York: Warner Books, 1985.

Porter, M. *Competitive Strategy*. New York: The Free Press, 1980.

Posner, B., Kouzes, J. and Schmidt, W. "Shared Values Make a Difference: An Empirical Test of Corporate Culture." *Human Resource Management*, 1985, 24(3), 293-309.

Quinn, J. "The Intelligent Enterprise: A New Paradigm." *The Executive*, 1992, 6(4), 48-63.

Quinn, J. *Strategies for Change: Logical Incrementalism*. Homewood, IL: Richard D. Irwin, Inc., 1980.

Raghuram, S. and Arvey, R. "Business Strategy Links with Staffing and Training Practices." *Human Resource Planning*, 1994, 17(3), 55-73.

Randolph, W., Sapienza, H., and Watson, M. "Technology-Structure Fit and Performance in Small Businesses: An Examination of the Moderating Effects of Organizational States." *Entrepreneurship Theory and Practice*, Fall, 1991, 27-41.

Robinson, R., Logan, J., and Salem, M., "Strategic Versus Operational Planning in Small Retail Firms." *American Journal of Small Business*, 1986, 10(3), 7-16.

Robinson, R. and Pearce, J. "Research Thrusts in Small Firm Strategic Planning." *Academy of Management Review*, 1984, 9(1), 128-137.

Robinson, R., Salem, M., Logan, J., and Pearce, J. "Planning Activities Related to Independent Retail Firm Performance." *American Journal of Small Business*, 1986, 19-26.

Robinson, P. and Sexton, E. "The Effect of Education and Experience on Self-Employment Success." *Journal of Business Venturing*, 1994, 9, 141-156.

Rocha, J. and Khan, M. "The Human Resource Factor in Small Business Decision Making." *American Journal of Small Business*, 1985, 10(2), 53-62.

Rokeach, M. *The Nature of Human Values*. New York: The Free Press, 1973.

Rosener, J. "Ways Women Lead." *Harvard Business Review*, November-December, 1990, 119-125.

Rosener, J., McAllister, D. and Stephens, G. "Leadership Study." Prepared for the International Women's Forum, June, 1990.

Roure, J. and Keeley, R. "Predictors of Success in New Technology Based Ventures." *Journal of Business Venturing*, 1990, 5, 201-220.

Rue, L. and Fulmer, R. "Is Long Range Planning Profitable?" *Proceedings of the Academy of Management*, Boston, 1973.

Rugman, A. and Verbeke, A. "Does Competitive Strategy Work for Small Business?", *Journal of Small Business and Entrepreneurship*, 1987,5(3), 45-60.

Rumelt, R. *Strategy, Structure and Economic Performance*. Boston: Harvard Graduate School of Business Administration, 1974.

Sandberg, W. "Strategic Management's Potential Contributions to a Theory of Entrepreneurship." *Entrepreneurship Theory and Practice*, Spring, 1992, 73-90.

Sandberg, W. and Hofer, C. "The Effects of Strategy and Industry Structure on New Venture Performance." *Frontiers of Entrepreneurship Research*, Babson College, 1986, 244-266.

Sapienza, H., Smith, K., and Gannon, M. "Using Subjective Evaluations of Organizational Performance in Small Business Research." *American Journal of Small Business*, 1988, 12(3), 45-54.

Schein, E. "The Role of the Founder in Creating Organizational Culture." *Organizational Dynamics*, 1983, 12 (1), 13-28.

Schendel, D. "Introduction to the Special Issue on Corporate Entrepreneurship." *Strategic Management Journal*, 1990, 11, 1-3.

Schneider, B. and Bowen, D. "The Service Organization: Human Resources Management is Crucial." *Organizational Dynamics*, 1993, 39-52.

Schuler, R. "Fostering and Facilitating Entrepreneurship in Organizations: Implications for Organization Structure and Human Resource Management Practices." *Human Resource Management*, Winter, 1986, 25(4), 607-629.

Schuler, R. "Personnel and Human Resource Management Choices and Organizational Strategy." *Human Resource Planning*, 1987, 10(1), 1-17.

Schuler, R. "Strategic Human Resource Management: Linking the People with the Strategic Needs of the Business." *Organizational Dynamics*, Summer, 1992, 21(1), 18-32.

Schuler, R. "Strategic Human Resource Management and Industrial Relations." *Human Relations*, 1989, 42(2), 157-184.

Schuler, R. "Systematic Human Resource Management.", working paper, New York University, 1988.

Schuler, R., Dowling, P, and DeCieri, H. "An Integrative Framework of Strategic International Human Resource Management." *Journal of Management*, 1993, 19(2), 419-460.

Schuler, R. and Jackson, S. "Linking Competitive Strategies with Human Resource Management Practices." *Academy of Management Executive*, 1987, 1(3), 207-219.

Schuler, R. and Jackson, S. "Linking Renumeration Practices to Innovation as a Competitive Strategy." *Human Resource Management Australia*, May, 1988, 6-21.

Schuler, R. and Jackson, S. "Organizational Strategy and Organization Level as Determinants of Human Resource Management Practices." *Human Resource Planning*, 1989a, 10(3), 125-140.

Schuler, R. and Jackson, S. "Determinants of Human Resource Management Priorities and Implications for Industrial Relations." *Journal of Management*, 1989b, 15(1), 89-99.

Schuler, R. and MacMillan, I. "Gaining Competitive Advantage Through Human Resource Management Practices." *Human Resource Management*, 1984, 23, 241-255.

Schuler, R. and Walker, J. "Human Resource Strategy: Focusing on Issues and Actions." *Organizational Dynamics*, 1990, 5-19.

Schwartz, H. and Davis, S. "Matching Corporate Culture and Business Strategy." *Organizational Dynamics*, 1981, 30-48.

Schwenk, C. and Shrader, C. "Effects of Formal Strategic Planning on Financial Performance in Small Firms: A Meta-Analysis." *Entrepreneurship Theory and Practice*, Spring, 1993, 53-64.

Sexton, D. and Kent, C. "Female Executives and Entrepreneurs: A Preliminary Comparison." *Frontiers of Entrepreneurship Research*, Babson College, 1981, 40-55.

Shirley, R. "Limiting the Scope of Strategy: A Decision Based Approach." *Academy of Management Review*, 1982, 7(2), 262-268.

Shortell, S. and Zajac, E. "Perceptual and Archival Measures of Miles and Snow's Strategic Types: A Comprehensive Assessment of Reliability and Validity." *Academy of Management Journal*, 1990, 33(4), 817-832.

Shrader, C., Mulford, C. and Blackburn, V. "Strategic and Operational Planning: Uncertainty, and Performance in Small Firms." *Journal of Small Business Management*, October, 1989, 45-60.

Shuman, J. and Seeger, J. "The Theory and Practice of Strategic Management in Smaller Rapid Growth Firms." *American Journal of Small Business*, Summer, 1986, 11(1), 7-18.

Slater, S. "The Influence of Managerial Style on Business Unit Performance." *Journal of Management*, 1989, 15, 441-455.

Slevin, D. and Covin, J. "The Competitive Tactics of Entrepreneurial Firms in High- and Low-Technology Industries." *Frontiers of Entrepreneurship Research*, Babson College, 1987, 87-101.

Small Business Administration (SBA). *1994 Handbook of Small Business Data*. Washington, D.C.: Government Printing Office, 1994.

Smith, B., Boroski, J., and Davis, G. "Human Resource Planning." *Human Resource Management*, 1992, 31(1), 81-93.

Smith, E. "Strategic Business Planning and Human Resources: Part I." *Personnel Journal*, August 1982a, 61, 606-610.

Smith, E. "Strategic Business Planning and Human Resources: Part II." *Personnel Journal*, September, 1982b, 61,680-682.

Smith, K., Gannon, M. and Sapienza, H. "Selecting Methodologies for Entrepreneurial Research: Trade-offs and Guidelines." *Entrepreneurship Theory and Practice*, Fall,1989, 39-49.

Smith, N., McCain, G. and Warren, A. "Women Entrepreneurs Really are Different: A Comparison of Constructed Ideal Types of Male and Female Entrepreneurs." *Frontiers of Entrepreneurship Research*, Babson College, 1982, 68-77.

The State of Small Business: A Report to the President, 1992, U.S. Government Printing Office, 1992.

The State of Small Business: A Report to the President, 1994, U.S. Government Printing Office, 1994.

Stoner, C. "Distinctive Competence and Competitive Advantage." *Journal of Small Business Management*, April, 1987, 25(2), 33-40.

Stonich, P. *Implementing Strategy: Making Strategy Happen*. Cambridge, Mass.: Ballinger, 1982.

Swiercz, P and Spencer, B. "HRM and Sustainable Competitive Advantage: Lessons from Delta Air Lines." *Human Resource Planning*, 1992, 15(2), 35-45.

Tannebaum, R. and Schmidt, W. "How to Choose a Leadership Pattern." *Harvard Business Review*, 1973, 162-180.

Tannen, D. *You Just Don't Understand.* New York: William Morrow and Company, Inc., 1990.

Taylor, F. *Principles of Scientific Management.* New York: Norton, 1911.

Thornburg, L. "Yes, Virginia, HR Contributes to the Bottom Line." *HR Magazine*, August, 1993, 62-63.

Thune, S. and House, R. "Where Long Range Planning Pays Off." *Business Horizons*, August, 1970, 81-87.

Tsui, A. and Gomez-Mejia, L. "Evaluating Human Resource Effectiveness." In L. Dyer (ed.) *Human Resource Management: Evolving Roles and Responsibilities.* Washington, D.C.: BNA Series, 1988, Chapter 1.5.

Ulrich, D., Geller, A. and DeSouza, G. "A Strategy, Structure, Human Resource Database: OASIS." *Human Resource Management*, 1984, 23(1), 77-90.

van Donk, D. and Esser, A. "Strategic Human Resource Management: A Role of the Human Resource Manager in the Process of Strategy Formation." *Human Resource Management Review*, 1992, 2(4), 299-315.

Variyam, J. and Kraybill, D. "Small Firms' Choice of Business Strategies." *Southern Economic Journal*, 1993, 60(1), 136-145.

Venkatraman, N. and Camillus, J. "Exploring the Concept of "Fit" in Strategic Management." *Academy of Management Review*, 1984, 9, 513-525.

Venkatraman, N. and Prescott, J. "Environment-Strategy Coalignment: An Empirical Test of Its Performance Implications." *Strategic Management Journal*, 1990, 11, 1-23.

Venkatraman, N. and Ramanujam, V. "Measurement of Business Performance in Strategy Research: A Comparison of Approaches." *Academy of Management Review*, 1986, 11(4), 801-814.

Walker, J. "The Building Blocks of Human Resource Management." *Human Resource Planning*, 1981, 179-187.

Weber, J. "The Relationship Between Managerial Value Orientation and Stage of Moral Development: Theory Development and Empirical Investigation with Behavioral Implications." Phd. D. Thesis, University of Pittsburgh, 1988.

Wiatrowski, W. "Small Businesses and Their Employees." *Monthly Labor Review*, October, 1994, 29-35.

444

444

444

Williams, M., Carter, N., and Reynolds, P.D. "Founding Strategy and Gender: Their Role in Predicting New Venture Failure Rates," working paper, Marquette University, 1993.

Wils, T and Dyer, L. "Relating Business Strategy to Human Resource Strategy: Some Preliminary Evidence." Paper Submitted to Academy of Management, 1984.

Wissema, J., Van Der Pol, H., and Messer, H. "Strategic Management Archetypes." *Strategic Management Journal*, 1980, 1, 37-47.

Wood, D. and LaForge, R. "The Impact of Comprehensive Planning on Financial Performance." *Academy of Management Journal*, September, 1979, 22(3), 516-526.

Wortman, M. "An Overview of the Research on Women in Management: A Typology and a Prospectus." In *Women in the Workforce*. New York: Praeger Publications, 1982.

Wortman, M. "Entrepreneurship: An Integrating Typology and Evaluation of the Empirical Research in the Field." *Journal of Management*, 1987, 13(2), 259-279.

Wright, P. "Human Resource Strategies: A Reconceptualization." Paper presented at The Academy of Management Meetings, 1986, Chicago.

Wright, P. and McMahan, G. "Theoretical Perspectives for Strategic Human Resource Management." *Journal of Management*, 1992, 18(2), 295-320.

Wright, P. and Parsinia, A. "Porter's Synthesis of Generic Business Strategies: A Critique." *International Management*, 1988, 30(3), 20-23.

Wright, P. and Snell, S. "Toward an Integrative View of Strategic Human Resource Management." *Human Resource Management Review*, 1991, 1(3), 203-225.

Zahra, S. "A Conceptual Model of Entrepreneurship as Firm Behavior: A Critique and Extension." *Entrepreneurship Theory and Practice*, Summer, 1993, 5-21.

Zahra, S. and Covin, J. "Business Strategy, Technology Policy and Firm Performance." *Strategic Management Journal*, 1993, 14, 451-478.

Index